with l

Sas Whaler
2009

Hooked at the Roots

Hooked at

the Roots

The Evolution of
Featherbone Communiversity

By Charles E. "Gus" Whalen, Jr.
with Phillip Rob Bellury

THE WARREN FEATHERBONE FOUNDATION

Hooked at the Roots
Published by The Warren Featherbone Foundation
615 F. Oak Street, Suite 500, Gainesville, GA 30501
Copyright © 2009 Charles E. "Gus" Whalen, Jr.

Book design and production:
Shock Design & Assoc., Inc.
Atlanta, GA, USA
shockdesign@mindspring.com

Printing: Matthews Printing, Gainesville, GA, USA

Binding: BindTech, Nashville, TN, USA

PICTURE CREDITS:

© Perry Daughtry: page 90
© Courtesy of Georgia Quick Start: page 41
© Larry Griffeth: pages 17, 28, 92-93, and 118
© 2008 Billy Howard: author photo and back cover photo on book jacket,
    pages xii, 24, 30, 38, 62, 72, 80, 94, 98, 102, and 106
© Linda Ingle: page 66
© Robb Maag: pages 35 and 65 (bottom)
© 2008 Sue Mabry: pages 74, 76, 78, 112, and 115
Michigan Historical Center: page 4
© Dana Miller: page 65 (top)
© Alexandra Picaret (National Park Service photo): page 18
© 2008 Dave Simpson: pages 48-55, 57-58, and 60
© Jon Sullivan: front cover jacket photo, pages ii-iii, and 42
© Three Oaks, MI city file photo: page 8
© 1997 Bob Tubbs: page 110
University of Southern Mississippi file photo, page 130

LC# 2008941405

10-Digit ISBN# 0-9655107-4-3
13-Digit ISBN# 978-0-9655107-4-5

First Edition

Contents

DEDICATION vii

FOREWORD ix

PREFACE—*The Spirit of Community Building* xiii

INTRODUCTION—*E.K. Warren, An Entrepreneur's Story* 1

CHAPTER 1—*A Blessing to Others* 9

CHAPTER 2—*Hooked at the Roots* 19

CHAPTER 3—*The Vision of Lanier Technical College* 31

CHAPTER 4—*Entrepreneurs: Dreams, Courage and Innovation* 43

CHAPTER 5—*INK: Imagining a New "Box"* 63

CHAPTER 6—*Brenau University: A Heritage of Innovation* 81

CHAPTER 7—*Featherbone Communiversity
from the Educator's Perspective* 93

CHAPTER 8—*A New Loaf* 111

CHAPTER 9—*What's Next for You?* 119

CHAPTER 10—*Final Thoughts, The Power to Give* 131

ABOUT THE AUTHOR 140

ACKNOWLEDGEMENTS 141

Dedication

This book is dedicated to the more than ten thousand employees of The Warren Featherbone Company whose character, creativity and productivity brought honor to the company and the community it served over the years.

It is also dedicated to my Featherbone Center partners whose vision makes Featherbone Communiversity possible today.

U.S. Congressman Nathan Deal

Foreword

September and October of 2008 presented all of us with some sobering realities. Within the span of a few weeks the stock market recorded unprecedented one-day losses and historic one-day gains. The United States Congress authorized $700 billion to rescue large banks and other institutions in an effort to stabilize the financial industry and unfreeze credit. The Finance Ministers of major industrialized nations met to coordinate their efforts to avoid an international depression. Millions of Americans saw the value of their savings and retirement accounts dramatically reduced. Home values plummeted and credit evaporated.

As I am writing, most of us are watching the economic indicators and awaiting the next Presidential address on the crisis. Therefore many of us are asking, "What's next?" How appropriate it is that my friend, Gus Whalen, asks this very question with his book, *Hooked at the Roots*.

Few individuals have the insight of Gus Whalen. In writing this book he draws on his rich ancestral heritage, his own experiences in an industry impacted by the evolving global marketplace, and his innate refreshing optimism, to provide a perspective on the hope springing from our connections with each other.

The Warren Featherbone Company, founded by Gus's great-grandfather, E.K. Warren, provides the canvas upon which a beautiful portrait has been painted. Its 126-year existence is unique in itself, but its ability to transform from making women's corsets in the 1800's to its most recent incarnation as a pioneer Communiversity is a saga worthy of examination.

What becomes clear is that success for a business or an individual must include persistence, adaptability, concern for others, and most of all the development of a sense of community. It is this story, emphasizing qualities not recorded on a balance sheet, which makes this book unique.

The establishment of the Featherbone Communiversity brings the vision of E.K. Warren into a modern focus. It embodies the dreams of the inventor and entrepreneur, the compassion of professional nurses, the concern for awakening the joy of learning in children, and the challenge of continuing to educate a diverse population. This storied corporation, and the philanthropic family that has guided it, illustrates the strength and resilience that resides in us all.

—NATHAN DEAL
U.S. CONGRESSMAN

Gus Whalen

Preface

THE SPIRIT OF COMMUNITY BUILDING

My good friend, Lee Lathrop of Vancouver, Washington, regularly asks me this question: "Gus, what's next for you?" I love the question because it implies there will be a next! A big part of the answer, of course, is *hope*. It's our choice.

In the 126-year history of The Warren Featherbone Company we, like most organizations, have been faced with that question many times. Today, what's next is Featherbone Communiversity. Another friend, Jim Whitlock, describes the "perfect life" as being lived in thirds.

First, we watch.
Then we do.
Then we teach, our highest calling.

And so it is with Warren Featherbone today; we are a part of teaching and learning.

Featherbone Communiversity in Gainesville, Georgia, is a new kind of community with roots going back to another time and place. It has evolved to become the home of collaborative, cross-generational learning through a unique alliance of educational institutions. To our knowledge, it is the first-of-its-kind learning community in the United States. It's a new way of thinking about education. A new system appears to be emerging through this community where the product is much greater than the sum of the parts. This system benefits the individual pieces as well as the whole. The potential benefits and opportunities are enormous.

Featherbone Communiversity's evolution is unlikely yet predictable when one looks at the DNA of the company from which the name is derived. In a sense, this is the story of the spirit of community building. It has had many manifestations and will no doubt continue to do so. In this story that spirit first touched the heart of my great-grandfather, E.K. Warren, of Three Oaks, Michigan. Many people have responded to that spirit and remarkable things have been achieved.

Sandra Day O'Connor writes, *"We don't accomplish anything in this world alone — and whatever happens is the result of the whole tapestry of one's life and all the weavings of individual threads from one to another that creates something."*

As you read this book, I believe you will see yourself as a part of this tapestry that can create something very special in your life and community. Perhaps this is a part of what's next for you too.

—Gus Whalen
Gainesville, Georgia
Spring 2009

E. K. Warren

E. K. Warren,
An Entrepreneur's Story

COMPILED FROM ISSUES OF *The Acorn*, THREE OAKS, MICHIGAN, 1919

*W*hen E.K. Warren was brought home in January 1919 to be buried in his beloved hometown of Three Oaks, Michigan, *The Acorn*, Three Oaks' weekly newspaper, reported that, "When the evening train which brought the funeral party drew into the local station, a thousand or more persons were present to greet in silent homage the remains of their old friend on this, his last homecoming." E.K. was a wealthy man by the end of his life, but according to the words of these friends who came to bid him farewell, he was the same person inside as the young twelve-year-old who came to Three Oaks in 1858 with his minister father, mother, and three older brothers. He was the same person as the young teen who dressed in used clothes brought from New England in the "missionary barrels." In the service the following day he was described as a "dutiful son, faithful husband, loving father, steadfast friend, Christian nobleman."

No one in the town disagreed.

On the day of his funeral he was remembered in as many different ways as the number of mourners who were there to pay their respects. The local community as well as friends from far away recalled the many occasions when his activities made local news, state news, and even national and international news.

E.K. started his career as a clerk in his father-in-law's dry-goods store, and after several years became a partner. Watching one day as a clerk worked to fix a piece of broken whalebone in a ladies' corset, he began to explore ideas to replace whalebone with some other sort of elastic material. On a visit to the Chicago Feather Duster Company, he saw large piles of turkey wing pointers being burned. Upon inquiry, he was told that the company had no use for them. His creative mind put the two dilemmas together and came up with a solution for both problems. The "worthless" turkey feathers could be used as a stay material to replace whalebone. Thus in 1883 the Warren Featherbone Company was formed.

Ten years were invested to develop the product, obtain capital to run the business, and find a market. According to local news, E.K. developed the business with great creativity, indomitable will, and unwavering confidence

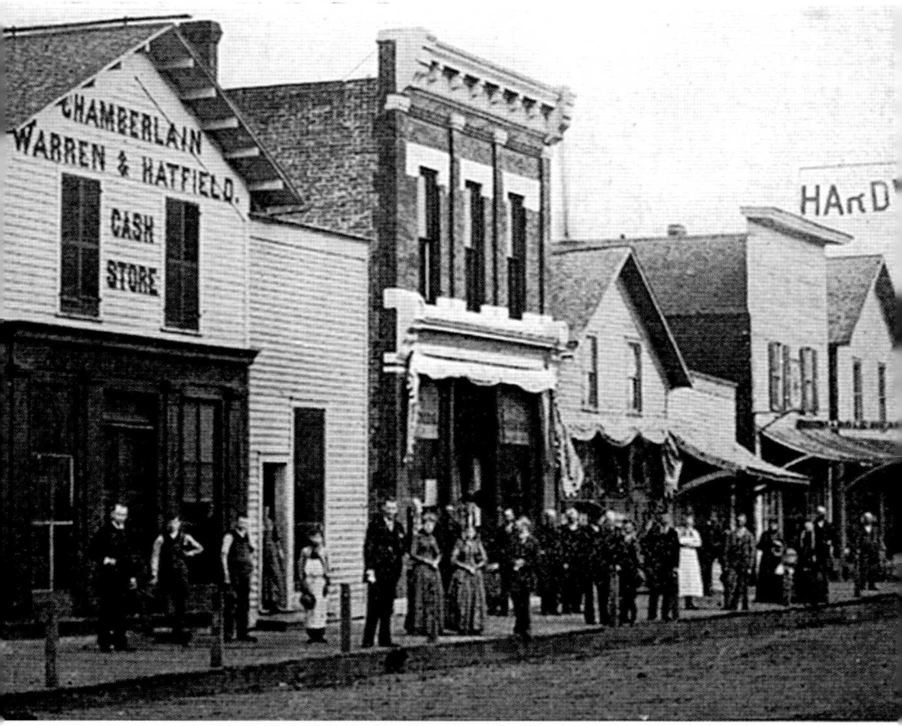

In 1890, Warren Featherbone offices were housed in the Chamberlain, Warren & Hatfield building on Elm Street in Three Oaks, Michigan.

in its ultimate success. The business, however, never over-shadowed his duties to family, church, and community.

He was remembered for being instrumental in seeing that Three Oaks had municipal water and a lighting plant, for hastening the building of a much needed depot, and for seeing that the county had safe and well-built roads.

He was remembered for establishing several business-es including E.K. Warren Grain Exchange, *The Acorn* newspa-per, Warren Whip Company, and two businesses that have thrived for over 100 years, the Warren Featherbone Company and the Bank of Three Oaks which became part of First Third Bank of Cincinnati, Ohio. In addition, Mr. Warren built the Congregational Church Parsonage in Three Oaks, and established the Chamberlain Memorial Museum.

The locals recalled fondly his organization of "Three Oaks Against the World." E.K. called a mass meeting of citizens and presented his proposal that Three Oaks compete against the rest of the nation to win the "Dewey Cannon," an ancient brass cannon taken by Admiral Dewey from Corregidor Island. The money raised would be used to fund a memorial for the fallen soldiers and sailors of the U.S. Maine. The award was based on money raised per capita, and Three Oaks won. A park was built for the cannon. E.K. invited President McKinley to come and help celebrate... and he came!

E.K. took his family to Palestine in 1901. The citizens

At the June 29, 1900 dedication ceremony, the Dewey Cannon was concealed with a large white tent. Upon the unveiling, the tent fell to the ground in pieces, revealing an eight-pointed red, white and blue star.

of Three Oaks remembered the excitement generated in their small community when a Stereopticon was presented showing pictures from this trip. According to the news of the day: "The Opera House was never more completely filled than on Friday night when about 1000 people responded to the invitations which had been sent out by Mr. Warren for the stereopticon entertainment." (*The first "PowerPoint" presentation!*) The photos were shown again for the children of Three Oaks and later to various Sunday School Conventions.

E.K. Warren was remembered as "the best friend the Michigan Sunday School Association ever had."

Who could forget 1904? E.K. was teacher of the adult class in the Three Oaks Sunday School and, simultaneously, Chairman of the Executive Committee of the World Sunday School Association and President of the World Sunday School Convention. In classic Warren style, E.K. chartered a steamship and took 817 delegates to the convention in Jerusalem.

He was remembered as "a man who did not just look about him. He looked far away into the future—a man of great vision." In 1878 he purchased Warren Woods (300 acres of virgin forest) and later Warren Dunes (a sand dune tract on

THE SAMARITAN MEDAL FOR PEACE AND HUMANITARIAN ACHIEVEMENT

*O*ne *of the presentations at the 1904 convention was made by the high priest of the Samaritan community. According to Mr. Warren, the presentation "was the most striking event of the convention". The Samaritan community descended from the ancient Kingdom of Israel and, in 1904, their numbers had declined to 168 people. Mr. Warren was taken with the problems of the Samaritans and helped them over a 17 year period by establishing schools for both boys and girls as well as providing financial support, including his purchase of manuscripts and artifacts for safekeeping.*

The Samaritan community has never forgotten Mr. Warren. In 2009, 105 years after that convention in Jerusalem, E.K. Warren is being presented posthumously The Samaritan Medal for Peace and Humanitarian Achievement.

Warren Dunes on Lake Michigan was leased to the state of Michigan by Edward K. Warren Foundation, "for the enjoyment of the citizens." The area is now known as Warren Dunes State Park.

Lake Michigan with 3,000 feet of shoreline). These were ultimately leased to the State of Michigan by the Edward K. Warren Foundation "for the enjoyment of the citizens of the state."* He was remembered as waking every morning with one thought in mind: That he might be "in some measure, at least, a blessing to others."

---

* The Warren Featherbone Foundation today has come full circle. See Final Thoughts, The Power to Give, at the end of this book

CHAPTER ONE

A Blessing to Others

*T*his story of community building began with the life of my great-grandfather, E.K. Warren. This is not so much my story. It is our story, in the sense that the principles illustrated in his life have been handed down to all of us through our families. The small town of Three Oaks, Michigan, still thrives today. In a 2008 *New York Times* article about Three Oaks, local resident, Allen Turner, is quoted: "I was there when the stores were empty. Now it's a thriving community with people interested in the idea of a cultural oasis. This is not a tourist stop. There are no fudge shops or T-shirt stores. It's a real community."

And that's what Mr. Warren has created—communities. It has been said that *the only profit a company ever really earns is the community it creates*. Throughout its history, Warren communities have been centered on businesses. The businesses have a life cycle and constantly evolve.

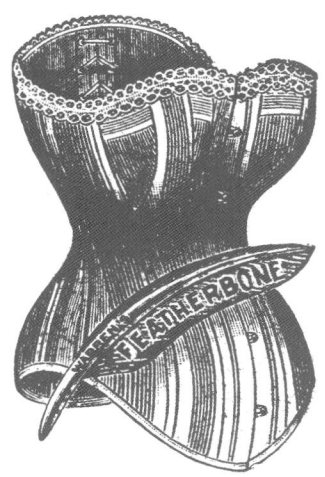

The products change, but the spirit, or DNA, of the company endures, and that spirit manifests itself in new enterprises over time—if we are open to it.

My work experience for 40 years has been in the Warren Featherbone Company. Mr. Warren founded the company in 1883 to produce a product known as Featherbone, a replacement for whalebone used as a stiffener in women's corsets. By using discarded turkey feather quills to make the Featherbone, E.K. Warren established himself as an early pioneer of what today is called green technology and sustainable business practices. Featherbone was a unique and wonderful product with hundreds of uses. It also established itself as a classic brand. You can still find "featherbone" in the dictionary even though you won't find Chevrolet, Pampers, or Tide. Unfortunately, it's listed right next to "feather-brain," but that's *not* part of this story.

In 1938, Warren Featherbone entered a major crisis, and it came at a time when it had virtually 100% of the Featherbone market and a brand to back it up... until...BF Goodrich developed a product with the U.S. Army known as

Koroseal, a seal against corro-
sion. Koroseal evolved into
plastic, one form looking like
vinyl shower curtains and the
other a variation that was
durable and flexible
like Featherbone —
and much less expen-
sive! Well, that and
changing fashions did it. We had
100% of a market that no longer existed. And we
had warehouses full of turkey feathers that no one needed.

According to Native American wisdom (Dakota), "If
the horse is dead, dismount." All of us love our dead horses; yet
we periodically must face reality and dismount. If we don't get
off, we become statues. But getting off is not the end. It simply
repositions us to move on. Here are just some of the products
Warren Featherbone has produced that invariably became
dead horses: Featherbone, sewing notions (seam binding, tapes,
and such), the first plastic baby pant, machine gun belts in
WWII, diaper bags, cosmetic bags, plastic raincoats, and shoe
covers for the Atomic Energy Commission. With each product, we eventually reached a point where we realized that the
horse was dead and it was time to dismount. Such was the case
when Koroseal came along.

The Chinese have a fascinating way of looking at crisis. Have you seen it? The Chinese see crisis as a normally occurring phenomenon, somewhat like growing pains. If you are alive, you are going to have them. Their graphic character for "crisis" is made up of two elements. The top figure translates literally, "dangerous," so crisis is in part a danger. However, we often miss the bottom element,  "opportunity." Crisis, then, is a "dangerous opportunity," but it is an opportunity only if we are open to the possibilities.

In 1938 that opportunity was to use Koroseal, our threat to survival, in a new way. Someone in the company looked at the features of Koroseal—waterproof, lightweight, and machine washable—and suggested that Warren Featherbone start making waterproof diaper covers for babies, which would replace "rubber pants" of the day. Did we want to change industries entirely? No! Did we? Yes, we did, and that ushered in nearly 70 years in a new field for

which we were not prepared, but one that made sense if you look at the DNA (spirit) of the company.

The baby clothes business was indeed very good for Warren Featherbone. Warren plastic baby pants were a hit in the market, with millions of dozens sold. And we had the

Warren brand too... until...the 1960's with the advent of disposable diapers from Playtex, Scott Paper Company, and the sales guerilla, Pampers. We tried to cover up Pampers with decorative "Pamper Covers," but to no avail. If the horse is dead, dismount.

We did dismount, and to our surprise discovered that we were simply in transition...yet still alive and breathing.

Speaking of transitions, for years I have been an avid pilot and one of my heroes is Bob Hoover, whose air show demonstrations in his twin-engine Aero Commander are unforgettable. The particular demonstration I remember most is one in which Bob stops both engines completely at 7000 feet, glides to a perfect landing, and taxies precisely to air show center. That's right. In this way, he "crashes" the airplane on purpose. His view of crashes is this: When you are in a crash (or think you are crashing), keep flying the airplane as far as you can into the crash. Don't panic and give up at 7000 feet—keep flying! Often what appears to us as an imminent crash is actually one of life's transitions. We get through them if we keep our head and are open to alternative solutions presented in the transition. These alternative solutions often take us to an even better place than we were before the "crash" began.

When plastic baby pants became obsolete and more modern manufacturing was required, Warren Featherbone purchased an infants apparel company, Alexis, Inc., of Atlanta, and moved all operations from Three Oaks, Michigan, to Gainesville, Georgia. That big transition was made by Charles Whalen, Sr., my father. Following his death in 1969, my stepmother Doris and I stepped in to run the family business. Over 10,000 wonderful associates became a part of the Warren Featherbone "community" in Gainesville from 1956 to 2005.

In 2005, however, we faced a gut-wrenching decision. For lower labor costs, U.S. production of apparel had largely moved offshore, initially to Mexico (NAFTA in 1992), Central America, and finally to China in 2005 as all trade restrictions with China were removed. Our decision seemed to be to either close the business or literally move physically from Georgia to China. History has shown that in all industries, large and small, the producer has to be on site to truly control production. Absent that, one is simply reselling someone else's work.

If the horse is dead....

The option we chose was to sell the business of our infantswear division, Alexis PlaySafe, to a firm in New Jersey. With assets to reinvest, we turned our sights toward another horizon. And on this horizon we saw a manifestation of something that had been a part of the Featherbone family of businesses from the start: education. Once again the company was not particularly prepared for this transition except by its DNA. That's what counted.

In 2005, The Warren Featherbone Company, along with local civic-minded individuals, organized Featherbone Center, LLC, to own the company's 127,000-square-foot manufacturing facility and adjacent property. Out of this, Featherbone Communiversity evolved into a campus with arms open to innovations in education. It provides collaborative, cross-generational learning through a unique alliance among educational institutions. We believe it is the first of its kind in the United States. The founding organizations are Brenau University Department of Nursing, Lanier Technical College Manufacturing Development Center (including Georgia Tech Enterprise Innovation Institute and the University of Georgia Small Business Development Center), and INK (Interactive Neighborhood for Kids). Located at the gateway to Gainesville, these organizations now serve as a new kind of learning community, and as E.K. Warren would say, "a blessing to others."

Is our first thought in the morning to be a blessing to others? Not always. For me it's usually, "Where's the coffee?" Yet this idea is very powerful. What if each morning our personal objective for the day was to be a blessing to others? Imagine what might happen. Perhaps, like E.K. Warren, those blessings given today will become our gifts to the future.

Featherbone Communiversity in Gainesville, GA.

The University of California explains that the sequoia seems to reach such extraordinary heights because of its ability to grow rapidly and continue growing into old age.

CHAPTER TWO

Hooked at the Roots

H ere's a question for you. What's 3,200 years old, still living, and 310 feet tall? Believe it or not, the tallest of the giant sequoias of the Sierra Nevada in Central California are that old and that tall. But there's more. Sequoias are unique. They grow only in about 75 groups, or groves, that are scattered over a single 260 mile strip in California less than 15 miles wide. They are remarkable also because of their *shallow* roots, 95% of which are no deeper than 3 feet. They survive because they grow in groves, roots interlocked below the surface, giving them a collective stability that endures for centuries.

And so it is with us.

As mentioned in the previous chapter, The Warren Featherbone Company sold the business of its infantswear division in 2005. Over its 125 years in different businesses, the company had faced other difficult decisions made for good business reasons. But this decision was particularly agonizing for me because of the jobs and the "community" that would be affected. The only real profit a company ever makes is the community it creates.

Once the decision to sell was made, Warren Featherbone itself faced the question "What's next?" What would continue? What would be discarded? What might we do with a 127,000 square foot manufacturing plant and more than seven acres of land located at the gateway to our city?

We listed the property with a local real estate firm and received a generous offer in the first hour of the first day the property was available for sale. In that moment we knew the company's legacy and community could be preserved only if we did not take that offer. And, much to the disbelief of the real estate company, we didn't. If we were not selling, what would be next for the property: warehousing, a call center, another outlet mall? Even though we said "no" to the sale, our real estate company helped us say "yes" to a new presence that would leverage Warren Featherbone's legacy of community building.

Warren Featherbone Company's financial advisor for 38 years has been P. Martin Ellard. He suggested forming a group to purchase the property, continue the Warren Featherbone legacy, and develop the property in a new form. At that time it was obvious that, though real estate was involved, this was about much more. Exactly what, however, was not clear.

The people we invited to join were community-minded, truly gifted in their profession, and each with significant life accomplishments. The group that became known as "Featherbone Partners" consisted of W.A. (Dub) Bagwell (attorney), P. Martin Ellard (CPA), Dr. Ralph Hopkins (radiologist), Dr. Nabil Muhanna (neurosurgeon), J.A. (Jim) Walters (banker), Philip Wilheit (Wilheit Packaging), and myself. The Warren Featherbone Company itself provided initial financial support. The "Featherbone Partners" were open to the idea that the facility (then known as Featherbone Center) could be dedicated to any number of uses. But one use that really captured us was an idea from Lanier Technical College which had previously expressed interest in creating a manufacturing incubator within Warren Featherbone. Our partners were open to the possibility, but had no strategic plan or concrete idea for how all this might occur.

In the pages that follow you will meet Dr. Keeta Wilborn, head of Brenau University's Department of Nursing. Entering Dr. Wilborn's office your eyes will be drawn to an embroidered pillow on a chair which states one of her favorite Zen proverbs: "Leap and the net will appear." The Featherbone Partners leapt, and the rest, as they say, is history.

"Leap and the net will appear."

The partners each had their own reasons for investing financial resources and talent into this project. For Warren Featherbone, it provided an opportunity to continue its legacy in a new way. As my friend Jim Whitlock reminded us, the "perfect life" is lived in three stages. First we watch. Then we do. Then we teach, our highest calling. Maybe Warren Featherbone could be reinvented now into the business of education. Could we create a new kind of learning community at Featherbone Center?

Once the decision to leap was made, an educational initiative began to take shape. The first stage had begun in 2004 when Lanier Technical College described their dream for a manufacturing incubator. Dr. Sheila Stille prepared a white paper of this dream, showing the need and the funding required to launch it. Dr Mike Moye, president of Lanier Tech, and Russell Vandiver, Vice President of Economic Development, got behind the effort and will always be remembered for their focus and persistence. Start-up funding was requested from local and federal sources. We asked the Hall County Commission members for a modest contribution and their response surprised us. They clearly saw the need for the incubator and suggested we double the request! The same request was made to the City of Gainesville and support was unanimously given. Both entities ultimately committed seven years funding. Then the area communities of Flowery Branch and Oakwood joined us, as did the Georgia Power Company. When the Appalachian Regional Commission provided a significant grant for infrastructure, we were in business. Lanier Tech's incubator, known as the Manufacturing Development Center, opened in July 2006.

In 2005 Dave Gines of Brenau University called me about a children's museum: INK, the Interactive Neighborhood for Kids. Dave was a Board member and INK needed larger quarters. At the time INK was located on the second floor of a former church building. I had not heard of INK or its founder, Sheri Hooper. Dave suggested a visit, and I remember being fascinated by the concept of creating a village for kids, ages 2-12, based on the real world. Much thought had been put into the captivating displays. I met Sheri Hooper and began to understand the passion and heart Sheri possesses. Following that visit I had no doubt that she and INK would be successful. In June 2006, INK moved out of 5,000 square feet in the church building into 12,000 square feet at Featherbone, and then grew to 27,500 square feet by 2008. Forty-eight thousand visitors were recorded at INK in 2007 alone. A learning community was taking shape.

The last stage of what is now Featherbone Communiversity fell into place in the fall of 2006. Brenau University, founded in 1878, five years before Warren Featherbone, has remained relevant and vital over the years and

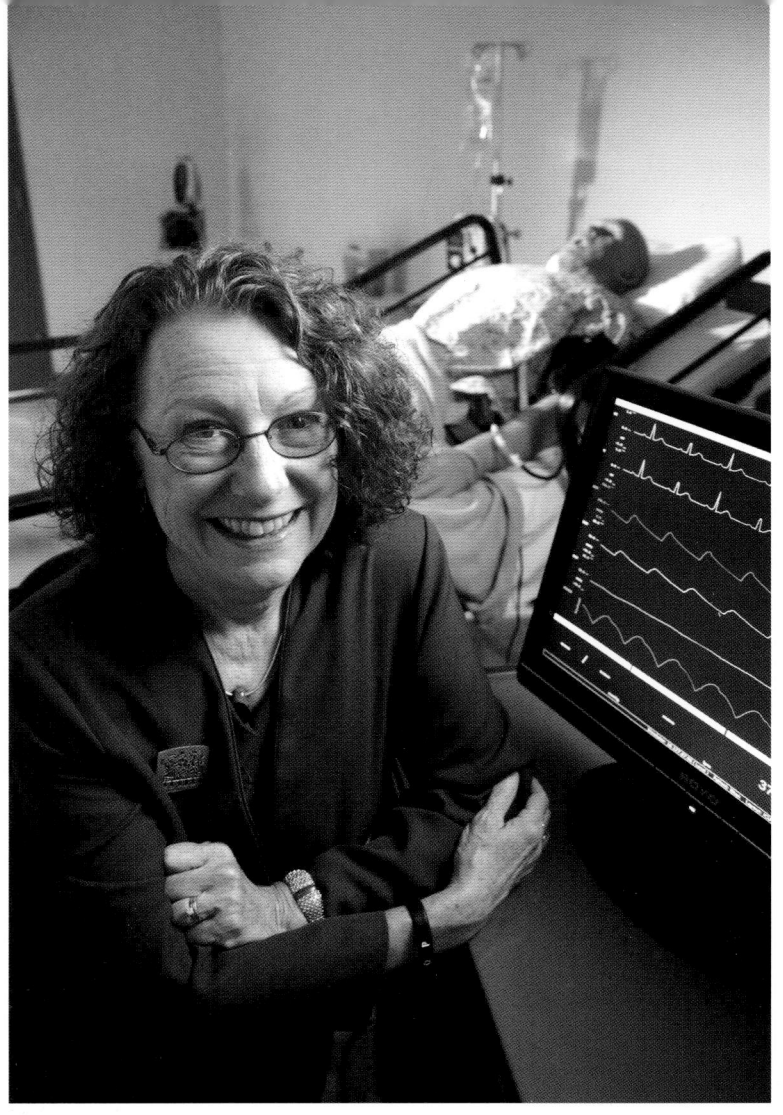

Dr. Keeta Wilborn is head of the Department of Nursing at Brenau University.

today educates more than 50% of the nurses in North Georgia. Brenau now faced the challenge of growing and relocating their Department of Nursing. Featherbone was suggested because of its location just off Interstate 985 along the primary entrance to Gainesville with ample parking and a blank canvas to create something extraordinary. A group of Brenau's leaders came to visit and toured 37,000 square feet that would become their new East Campus. Dr. Wayne Dempsey, Brenau's CFO, first had the vision, and we all saw the challenges and opportunities. Dr. Keeta Wilborn, head of the Department of Nursing (and owner of the embroidered pillow), made a comment as we left the building that day that I will never forget. "I like being located next to children at INK." As events have unfolded, nursing students regularly visit INK as part of their education in nursing.

Garland Reynolds, one of the south's most creative architects, soon went to work with skillful builder Carroll Daniel Construction Company to create an amazing transformation. An elegant new portico with white Tuscan columns in the Italian Renaissance style was added to the front of the building. The classrooms, labs, and auditorium were designed to be extra wide with curved walls at corners to make them appear shorter and easier to navigate. Captivating art from Brenau students, faculty and others added to the finished elegance of the space. First classes for nursing students were held in August 2007, and now a complex for theatre and dance instruction has been added.

Brenau University, Lanier Technical College, and INK were coming together at Featherbone as more than just tenants co-located in a building. There was a new form evolving—a learning community—but we didn't know what to call it.

For some time the Warren Featherbone Foundation had been working with Marsha Hopkins as a creative advisor on the subject of emerging organizational forms. In the summer of 2006 she introduced us to August (Gus) and Joanne Jaccaci of New Gloucester, Maine. Gus and Joanne have worked with leaders throughout the world to help them envision and architect an ideal future for themselves and their enterprises. They are authors, speakers, respected visionaries, and social inventors.

When we met, I described to Gus what was "growing" at Featherbone. He said that it sounded like a "communiversity." Though the term had been used previously, it has a new meaning as it is evolving for us. Featherbone Communiversity has three principle characteristics of learning:

· Real-time learning...
· in a collaborative setting...
· that is intergenerational (ages 2 to 92 in one facility)...

On January 3, 2007, Warren Featherbone Foundation held a "Conversation with Gus and Joanne Jaccaci" for 38 community leaders to "explore the promise of the communiversity concept for the present, and ways that it might lead us to whole-community learning in the future". This was followed by a Visioning Meeting for local leaders on May 6, 2007, led by master educator Bill Hale, one of the founders of the University of Georgia's Center for Continuing Education. What came from that meeting, among other things, was the notion that physical resources could be shared internally with each other and externally for the whole community.

On October 18, 2007, Featherbone Communiversity was officially dedicated in a packed auditorium with the keynote address provided by Georgia's Lt. Governor Casey Cagle. What we all witnessed was the birth of a learning community. Organizationally, it is unique in that there is no central source of funding. Each entity brings its financial resources and operates its own programs. In the process, it shares resources (physical and intellectual) with the others, and collaborates when appropriate. The connections are endless. To

Also present at the dedication was Georgia Lt. Gov. Casey Cagle, who said in watching The Warren Featherbone Company over the years, he has seen successes that have made the community proud. "Now that The Warren Featherbone Company has been reinvented, it will continue to carry on the legacy of fostering new entrepreneurship within the community."

The auditorium at Featherbone Communiversity has become a favorite learning environment for teachers, students and the larger community.

Featherbone
COMMUNIVERSITY

name a few, nurses train at INK, a medical device manufacturer at Lanier Tech works with Brenau, interns come into all three programs from local high schools, adult learning is scheduled for both Brenau and Lanier Tech, INK and Lanier Tech house a resource center for day-care center operators and workers.

Featherbone Communiversity has become a new model for learning communities. There will be others for sure. But what happened in Gainesville started on a leap of faith. Yes, Warren Featherbone's infantswear business had been sold. But that "community" didn't leave because the larger community, hooked at the roots with us, wouldn't let it go. A new even more powerful community has emerged. We are only beginning to realize its potential.

In your life, what connections are there for the important work and service in your future? They are probably closer than you realize. From our experience, it helps to remain open and take that leap of faith. And, of course, leaps of faith are easier when you are hooked at the roots with family, friends, and community who support you.

❧

When we try to pick out anything by itself,
we find it hitched to everything else in the universe.
— JOHN MUIR

Dr. Michael D. Moye, President of Lanier Technical College

CHAPTER THREE

The Vision of
Lanier Technical College

❦

Although business and technology incubator programs have been around since 1959, not much was heard about them until the late 1990s when the fabled dot-com boom and bust drew a lot of attention in their direction. By then, thankfully, business incubators were well-established community-based initiatives, and were largely unaffected by the failures of the dot-com "gold rush." Business and technology incubators proliferated in the '80s and spread to the UK, Europe and beyond. From then until now, most have been fueled by economic development initiatives, local and regional government, colleges and technical schools, and angel investment groups. When those entities have worked collaboratively to provide support to start-up companies, the success rates have been phenomenal; one estimate is a whopping 87% for those companies that have graduated from an incubator program.

Every business incubator program differs to some degree from the next one, but the benefits to the community are the same. As start-up businesses succeed and expand, jobs and wealth are created. Successful companies in a given industry encourage other companies in that industry (industry clusters) to locate nearby. Local economies are stimulated by an environment that encourages and nurtures entrepreneurial business owners. As companies grow, they support other service industries in the local economy. The list goes on, but the bottom line is that over time successful incubator programs are a boon to the economy and help to revitalize the community.

Unlike federal business support programs, which are mandated to provide services to any new or existing business at any stage of development, business incubators typically select qualified companies that are in the very early or start-up phase. While most programs offer physical space and shared administrative services, the more important resources include business advice and counseling, marketing help, networking, access to investment capital, and a host of other practical and intangible resources. Programs that are tied to colleges and technical schools offer the added advantages of training and skill development, technology development, and other higher education resources.

The average success rate for businesses overall is low.

Estimates vary from one study to the next but it is generally accepted that less than half survive beyond four years. So why do graduates from business and technology incubator programs enjoy such a high success rate? What's the secret? And what does any of that have to do with Featherbone Communiversity?

Several years ago, Dr. Michael D. Moye, president of Lanier Technical College in Oakwood, Georgia, visited a business incubator program in Dallas, Texas. The Bill J. Priest Institute for Economic Development first opened its Business Incubator Center in 1990 to offer new business entrepreneurs a place where they could learn how to do business while they conducted business. Dr. Moye was so impressed with the concept that he was inspired to create a manufacturing incubator program that would serve the North Georgia community. While other business incubator programs were already operating successfully in other regions of the state, none were operating in the Gainesville-Hall County area. He recognized the need for one and took action.

Today, Lanier Tech serves nearly 30,000 students through long-term degree and diploma programs, as well as a multitude of economic development and adult literacy non-credit programs. The college is doing its part for the region by offering these programs to train and educate a skilled workforce. In recent years, however, Dr. Moye and others involved in education watched as manufacturing jobs were declining and efforts to attract existing manufacturers to the region were losing ground. What was needed was a manufacturing development program that would birth new companies and provide real-world assistance to get those new companies established and, ultimately, help to create new manufacturing job opportunities in the community. But to turn the idea into reality, Lanier Tech would need to engage in a series of developmental steps: a feasibility study, funding development, and a search for a building in which to locate.

"That's when we started talking about creating a business and manufacturing incubator at Featherbone," Dr. Moye recalls. "At that point, in early 2005, we were still conceptual but we knew it was a good idea. The Warren Featherbone Company building was coming available, and it seemed like a feasible location. In June of that year we held a luncheon to introduce the idea and invited people from the community. We had very good attendance, heard remarks from the mayor and other community leaders, and the reception was extremely favorable. Knowing the community was behind us gave us the confidence to march forward."

To get the ball rolling, Lanier Tech engaged the consulting services of Dr. Sheila Stille, who immediately saw the potential and accepted the challenge to "package" the concept for presentation to targeted partners. As a former direc-

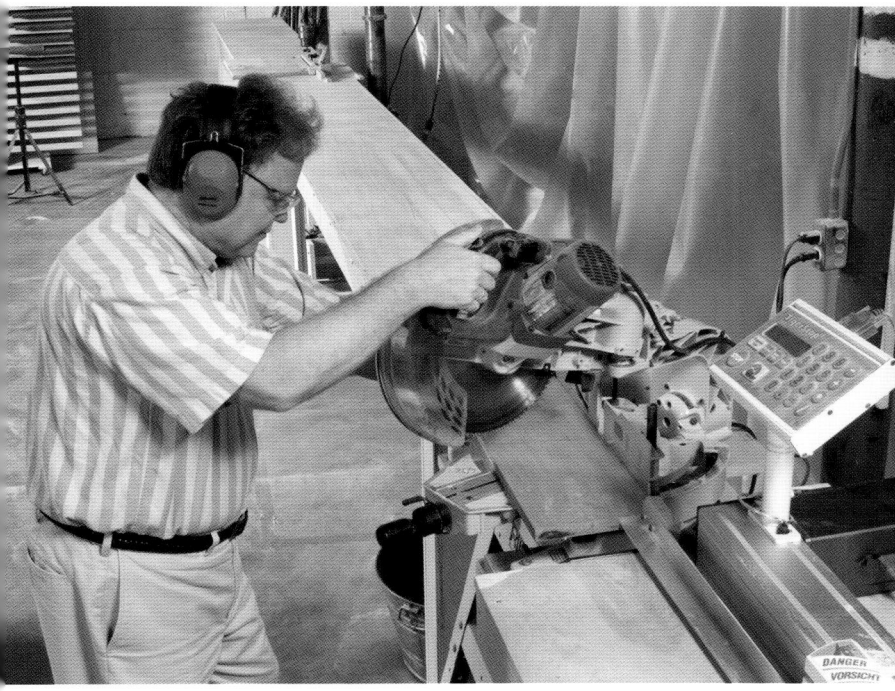

Paul Franklin, a Manufacturing Development Center entrepreneur

tor of planning and resource development with the Technical Colleges of Georgia, Dr. Stille already understood the dynamics of engaging and bringing together the appropriate stakeholders in the community including chambers of commerce, industrial and economic development organizations, local governments, and investor groups. She went to work on developing a white paper that explored the need and explained in detail the advantages and opportunities, as well as the steps necessary to bring the program to fruition.

Among the findings revealed in the white paper was the importance of developing "the spirit and 'know-how' of start-up entrepreneurs." As Dr. Moye points out, many entrepreneurs became proficient as employees and then made the leap into their own business ventures.

"Entrepreneurship is important because it eventually grows jobs," Dr. Moye explains. "At Lanier Tech, we teach people how to do things with their minds and their hands, but many of them are potential entrepreneurs who will start businesses. A high percentage of employees go on to start their own businesses, and most new jobs are created by small businesses and entrepreneurs. So one thing we always need to do in a community is to support small businesses. And that's what we envisioned for the Manufacturing Development Center (MDC): a dynamic opportunity to help entrepreneurs establish successful businesses in the region."

Working as a team, and armed with Dr. Stille's feasibility study and passion for seeing the idea succeed, Lanier Tech and Featherbone Communiversity made presentations and refined the concept to gain support and financing. Ultimately, they were successful in securing a federal grant and additional funding from city and county government to initiate the program. In January, 2006, the Manufacturing

Development Center (MDC) opened at Featherbone Communiversity as the new organization's first collaborative partner and tenant in the building. Lanier Tech's MDC provides services to fifteen entrepreneurs whose businesses span a broad range of manufacturing, technology, and service industries. The concept has become reality, and the community is being served.

What makes the MDC at Featherbone Communiversity even more special is the collaboration it enjoys with other people and organizations located there. Included in that are onsite resources from Georgia Tech and the University of Georgia, whose business and technology counselors advise clients on practical issues such as developing business plans, engineering, licensing and patenting, marketing and financing. It is a huge advantage for clients to have access to all that knowledge and assistance under the same roof, and the results have already proven to be rewarding. In other words, it's working!

"One of the reasons it works," says Dr. Moye, "is because of the natural synergy that had been born there without anyone saying they had to work together. All the agencies involved are fighting to help the businesses succeed, and the businesses are receiving the kind of practical help, encouragement and accountability that is so critical for entrepreneurs trying to get a business off the ground."

Russell Vandiver, Vice President for Economic Development at Lanier Technical College, with Dr. Michael D. Moye.

"The other exciting thing about being at Featherbone Communiversity is the collaborative learning that takes place between people at the MDC and the other organizations located there," says Russell Vandiver, Vice President for Economic Development at Lanier Technical College. "We're working together with both INK and Brenau Department of Nursing in ways that we didn't foresee until we all got here. It's great to know that we are involving people at every age, from kids who might catch a vision for their future, all the way up to older adults trying to bring their products to market. Who knows, we may be grooming the next Bill Gates here."

Dr. Carroll Turner, the director at the MDC, agrees. As the person most responsible for oversight of the program, he understands both the "nuts and bolts" and the other intangibles that make new business entrepreneurs successful.

"Passion is probably the most important thing," he says. "You need to have a good idea, a good business plan, and a host of other practical things in place, but it's passion that will drive an entrepreneur to stick with it and work hard to become successful."

Without a doubt, there is a high degree of passion and entrepreneurial energy at the MDC. You can feel it when you walk through the center and meet the people involved. It's a spirit of collaboration, learning and growing together. In a way, it's like visiting the labor and delivery ward at a hospital, because the MDC is at heart a birthing center for businesses. For those of us who worked at Featherbone Communiversity when it was a place for manufacturing baby clothes, it seems as though we've come full circle. To know that we are still helping "newborns" is encouraging. It's also rewarding to know that the "spiritual DNA" that began with E.K. Warren in Three Oaks,

Michigan, in the 1800s and found a home in Gainesville, Georgia, in the 1950s, still resides there. That Lanier Tech and the MDC were the first to become part of Featherbone Communiversity seems to be a perfect sequel to what has always been a part of the Featherbone legacy.

"The idea of locating the program at Featherbone Communiversity made a lot of sense to me," Dr. Stille recalls. "But it was never about the real estate; it was about a good idea, a partnership that would make a big difference in the community. The Warren Featherbone Company has always embraced the community, and I believe the community has always embraced Featherbone. There's a nurturing relation-ship that's happened there over the years, so the idea of bringing Lanier Tech's manufacturing development center there seemed like a perfect fit, an ideal location to support entrepreneurs and give birth to new companies. There was an openness to work together, whatever direction it took, and it was never about the real estate."

But it was the vision of Lanier Tech that ultimately led us to communiversity. Where can your vision take you? Are you sitting on an idea that can change the world or improve your community in a real way? It's easy to say, "I am only one person." But you *are* one — with unique talents and abilities. Can you make a difference? If you seriously ask the question, the answer will come.

*Georgia Manufacturing Appreciation Week Luncheon—
celebrating its 15th anniversary in 2009.*

Historically, The Warren Featherbone Company and the Technical College System of Georgia (formerly the Georgia Department of Technical and Adult Education) have partnered to promote manufacturing in Georgia. Their most successful effort in that regard has been Georgia's Manufacturing Appreciation Week, which held its first Awards Luncheon in 1995 in Macon, Georgia. The Boeing plant in Macon was the first recipient of the Manufacturer of the Year Award, and the CEO at the time, Phil Condit, received the award in front of 122 people, forty of whom were employees of The Warren Featherbone Company. Since then, under the guiding leadership of the Technical College System of Georgia, the initiative has enjoyed phenomenal growth; attendance at the 2008 awards banquet was more than 1500.

*Entrepreneurs and small businesses are the
courageous wealth generators that have made
and will continue to make our economy strong.
They are the only ones who really can.*

— Gus Whalen

CHAPTER FOUR

Entrepreneurs: Dreams, Courage and Innovation

⊷⊶

America has a continuing crisis that affects all of us. That crisis is the erosion of our industrial base and the hemorrhaging of important jobs and skills in manufacturing. The numbers are staggering and the danger is very real.

In 2007 (the last full year reported as of this writing), the United States trade deficit hit $731 billion. The trade deficit with China alone was $256 billion (compared to $83 billion in 2001). What this means is that the United States continues to produce $2 billion less in goods and services each day than it buys abroad. As a country we borrow new money or sell assets to make up the difference. This is an important part of our $ 2.44 trillion net foreign debt now owed to foreign investors. China and Japan are our largest creditors.

The creditors are becoming uneasy. Joseph Stiglitz, Nobel Prize winner and former chief economist of the

World Bank states, "The untold story here is that foreign investors are no longer willing to finance American debt. They now want equity." Recent sales of U.S. assets to foreign investors prove his point. A partial list of these sales includes Anheuser Busch, Genentech, Alcon, Barr Pharmaceuticals, Millennium Pharmaceuticals, Merrill Lynch, DRS Tech, Philadelphia Consolidated, APP Pharmaceuticals, the GM Building, the Chrysler Building, and the General Electric Appliance Division.

In 2008, the ailing economy in the U.S. was addressed in part by a $152 billion "stimulus" package. We all received our checks in the mail, but where did that money come from? We borrowed it from China and others. With that money we often went to stores like Wal-Mart to buy foreign manufactured products which supported manufacturing jobs and economies of other nations, but not ours.

To make matters worse, along with our soaring $14.5 trillion in household debts for mortgages, credit cards, health, education, and so on, all of us in the United States collectively owe an additional $10 trillion in federal government debt. (This does not include the historic $700 billion economic bailout of 2008.) To repay this federal debt, our country is borrowing each year to bridge the widening gap between government revenue and spending. It's hard to comprehend these figures. Denis Hayes is an environmental advocate, proponent of solar power, and author. He has studied and speaks to the national debt because that debt affects our nation's ability to deal with every other issue from protecting the environment to terrorism. As he says, "A bankrupt nation is a weak nation." Here's how Denis Hayes sizes up our debt:

ZEROES ARE IMPORTANT

The combined American household and federal debt is $24 trillion.

A million seconds ago was last week.

A billion seconds ago, Richard Nixon resigned the presidency.

A trillion seconds ago was 30,000 BC.

Zeroes are important. A million seconds ago was last week. A billion seconds ago, Richard Nixon resigned the presidency. A trillion seconds ago was 30,000 BC, and early humans were using stone tools.

Again, our combined household and federal debt is $24 trillion!

Manufacturing is a key component of the trade deficit. In 2007, the manufacturing trade deficit was $499 billion (compared to $304 billion in 2001). Nearly 75% of our manufacturing industries recorded trade deficits. We are losing manufacturing jobs at an astonishing rate of 2,000 jobs per day. That means over 3 million manufacturing jobs have vanished since 2001. And with each manufacturing job lost goes an additional 1 $^1/_2$ support jobs. As we lose these jobs and the skills represented, we lose our nation's ability to create economic wealth through manufacturing. Many believe, in fact, there are only three ways to create economic wealth: agriculture, extraction (mining, drilling, and such) and manufacturing.

If I have learned anything, it is this: Everything is connected. When we lose manufacturing we lose our ability to create wealth. As a nation we therefore have less because we produce less. This leads to loss of important jobs that significantly diminishes the once-powerful middle class. As we lose our middle class, we are increasingly polarized into "haves" and "have-nots." Most importantly, as we lose our middle class, we lose our democracy.

What can we do to reverse this trend? Where is there hope? Our history has shown the power of Yankee ingenuity and innovation. There is no shortage of great ideas for manufacturing in the United States. As you have read, Warren Featherbone Company no longer manufactures products per se. Our legacy in manufacturing, however, is more important than ever. Through Lanier Technical College and the Manufacturing Development Center at Featherbone Communiversity we are enabling a whole new generation of manufacturing entrepreneurs—and they will change our world!

Entrepreneurs and small businesses are the courageous wealth generators that have made and will continue to make our economy strong. They are the only ones who really can. The vast majority of all businesses in the United States are small family businesses. Dr. Joe Astrachan is the Executive Director of the nationally known Cox Family Enterprise Center at Kennesaw State University in Kennesaw, Georgia. Dr. Astrachan says flatly, "Without family business, there would be no economy."

Our job is to support and encourage these entrepreneurs in every way we can. Today fifteen new businesses have started and are growing in the Lanier Technical College Manufacturing Development Center at Featherbone Communiversity. (Twenty entrepreneurial businesses are in line to enter.) They provide over 60 new jobs and create products important for all of us. And they will continue to grow, one day graduating from the Manufacturing Development Center, making way for new businesses and innovations of tomorrow.

So, how do entrepreneurs see the world? What drives them? What do they seek? We asked the founding entrepreneurs of the Manufacturing Development Center (MDC) to share their views in a round-table discussion. Here's what they told us:

PAUL FRANKLIN, RESIDENTIAL TECHNOLOGY, INC.

With two masters degrees in Electrical Engineering and Computer Science, Paul had the skills and aptitude to succeed in the corporate environment. But his passion has always been carpentry and making things that have lasting value to people. He started Residential Technology initially from his home and has since located at the MDC where he has developed a market niche constructing residential and commercial cabinetry at a Lexus level of quality.

"Input from Georgia Tech personnel, Carroll Turner, and others here has been invaluable, including help with OSHA, floor and equipment layout, and processes. From financial, to employee relations, to setting prices, to marketing, we have gotten terrific advice and mentoring. Also, access to classes onsite has really helped; we've taken marketing, cash flow and Quickbooks classes that were excellent. I can't think of a better environment for starting and growing a small business. I don't think we would have survived if we had stayed in our basement. "

—PAUL FRANKLIN

RICK GARRETT, BETTER HEALTHCARE PRODUCTS

Rick is growing a bio-medical company that among other things is developing a patient positioning device in conjunction with Brenau Department of Nursing, also located at Featherbone Communiversity. That product will help solve an ongoing problem for nurses who experience back injuries from trying to turn patients in their beds. For one year Rick commuted from Dalton, Georgia, eighty miles away, to take advantage of Lanier Tech's MDC and get his company off the ground.

"I haven't minded the commute so much. To be an entrepreneur, you have to be willing to put everything on the line including your time and your income. You do everything you have to do to make it happen. I never let fear or common sense get in the way; I just go ahead and do it. As sure as there are high points, there will be low points in the business, but if you believe in it, you gotta' do it!"

—RICK GARRETT

BEN LICHTENWALNER, BIOTRAUMA
RYAN SAWYER, BIOTRAUMA

Ben and Ryan are both young veterans of the United States Marine Corps and are professionals in biohazard remediation. BioTrauma specializes in cleaning and repairing homes and offices that have been the scene of deaths, accidents and crimes. Their training and experience allows them to deal effectively with the daunting task of crime scene clean-up, but with a sensitivity and respect for the families who are left to pick up the pieces after a tragedy has occurred.

"*I was raised middle class and taught that the definition of success was going to work at a large company, but it made sense to be the one in control of my own future. I never enjoyed the day-to-day thing at other companies, and I am so much happier controlling my own future. This is not a business that my children are likely to follow me in, but I will encourage them to be entrepreneurs. There are universal things in business that I can share with them, knowledge that will help them make the jump if that's what they decide to do.*"

—BEN LICHTENWALNER

"I feel that God had a plan for me and Ben to be on the same assignment in Iraq at precisely the same time. I always thought I would be a high school coach, but I would not change a thing. This is what I'm supposed to do."

—Ryan Sawyer

SEAN AND LORI JOHNSEN, ICARD NOW

Sean and his wife, Lori, have developed the icard concept to augment their commercial printing business. Essentially, the icard is a personal business card, digitally printed in full color at a remarkably affordable cost. Sean has discovered a growing marketing niche, as described by *Time* magazine which refers to the icard concept as a non-business business card. Sean and Lori's operation employs the most advanced digital printing equipment available today.

"Being an entrepreneur is pretty much on target for me. I expected to enjoy being free from ties to a corporate desk, and that's what I found. What I didn't expect was spending more time with my family as we work together in the business. It takes courage to be an entrepreneur. You have to get out there in front and you may have friends or family who say you're not going to make it. And you can't be running away from something to start a business; it needs to be something you are running toward. It's about desire, passion, knowledge of the product... and not a get-rich scheme."

—SEAN JOHNSEN

Susan Rettig, Rettig Third Party Logistics

Susan never planned on being an entrepreneur, but started the business after her son suffered a back injury. She purchased a box truck for him to operate and over time the company evolved into the bustling business it is today. Rettig is a third party logistics provider specializing in dry and refrigerated truckload transportation services.

"Ours is a family business, but it wasn't originally intended that way. I started the business for my oldest son, but as we grew my other children came in one at a time. I think we've been successful because we stress honesty and integrity with our customers and our vendors. My philosophy is that it's not your money until you pay everybody you owe."

—Susan Rettig

Dave Simpson, Simpson Custom Photography

Dave left a family business that was founded by his father and started his own custom photography company. Simpson Custom Photography provides photography for a wide range of applications including aerial, architectural, commercial, portraits and more.

"There were 15 employees at my father's business, so there were a lot of people to handle different aspects of the business. Now I'm the sole employee and I've learned there's an overwhelming amount of details to handle. But if you find out what you're passionate about, you'll find out how to do it. Being an entrepreneur means you can't always count on a steady paycheck, but that is both a caution and an opportunity. The potential is unlimited; it just depends on how far you want to take it.

—Dave Simpson

ED FICKEY, WAKE UP OUTDOORS

Ed is an inventor who began work on a deer stand elevation device after his son was injured playing football. The platform was a way for him to still enjoy one of their favorite pastimes, deer hunting. Today, Ed's son is working with him as they continue to develop the product for a number of other applications and bring it to market.

"The development part of bringing a new product to the market is exciting. This was the first time I have worked through the whole process of design, patenting, and marketing. There are a lot of liability and legal questions, and other issues that I have to be concerned about because there's no one else doing it. I encourage others to pursue their dreams, but to be sure they have a plan, and double the time you think it will take to develop it."

—ED FICKEY

The entrepreneurs at the Lanier Tech Manufacturing Development Center represent the hope for future generations. As their businesses grow and expand the economy, the entire community is the beneficiary. Their success is our success. Each new business owner quickly testifies to the fact that the MDC has been a major contributor to their successes, and they all share a high regard for the people who provide them with advice and counsel as they grow their companies.

"I looked all over for something like this, and the people at Georgia Tech finally referred me here," says Rick Garrett. "I found everything I needed right here, and I was able to get my product inside a hospital for testing with help from Dr. Turner. It's a unique situation; I don't think the people of Gainesville know it's here."

"I was beating down the door to get it," admits Ben Lichtenwalner. "Having the practical resources here at the Center is great, but on top of that we get technical assistance, mentoring, help with the business plan... I don't know where we'd be if we weren't here, but we would not be nearly as far along as we are."

While they all agree they are doing what they are supposed to be doing in their businesses, the entrepreneurs at Lanier Tech's Manufacturing Development Center also share in the belief that starting one's own business may not be

Dr. Carroll Turner, Director of Lanier Tech's Manufacturing Development Center at Featherbone Communiversity

for everyone, that the road can sometimes be very rocky and the challenges difficult.

"This is a place where you learn how to pray," says Ed Fickey. "If you don't know how before you come, you will learn here. I suggest you learn beforehand, and then once you do, truly listen to the response."

Amen.

Dr. Carroll Turner

*A*fter a remarkable career in management positions at both GE and Hewlett-Packard, Dr. Carroll Turner, Director of Lanier Tech's Manufacturing Development Center, certainly earned the right to spend his post-retirement days on the golf course or on his boat in the Bahamas. And he did for a while, until he learned that the leisurely lifestyle didn't suit him. With 35 years of experience in corporate America and as an entrepreneur, he also knew that he still had something to offer. So Dr. Turner returned to his real passion – innovation in business. He specialized in bringing innovative medical devices to the market, and among other notable achievements developed the first hand-held ultra-sound device. While he still keeps his hand in his medical device company, Turner Medical, Dr.

MANUFACTURING DEVELOPMENT CENTER

Turner now devotes his time and energies to the clients at the MDC. And he's already earned a reputation as the number one "go-to guy" for advice and counsel.

"I learned from the masters," he says, noting his years working closely with the founders of Hewlett-Packard, Bill Hewlett and Dave Packard. "They started their business in a garage during the Great Depression and look where it went. While I worked there, I learned what it meant to be an entrepreneur within the corporation. I picked up a lot of business practices that lead to success, so what I do here is try to match the entrepreneurs' ideas and innovations with good practices so they can succeed."

Dr. Turner predicts that the MDC numbers will grow significantly each year and that the key ingredient to the success of those businesses is passion.

"You have to have that fire in your belly, and you have to have a bias for action," he says, "a desire to make things happen. You can't just wait for it to happen. And I also believe it helps to have a good understanding of Judeo-Christian values, which can help business owners avoid many problems. Learning values and ethics in business is as important as learning good business skills."

BRENAU UNIVERSITY IDEA DEVELOPMENT CENTER

DR. WILLIAM S. LIGHTFOOT
*Dean, Brenau School of Business
and Mass Communication*

*T*he Brenau University Idea
Development Center partners
with Lanier Tech and is physically located in the Manufacturing
Development Center.

"Ideas are abundant—espe-
cially for budding entrepreneurs. The challenge is in first
helping the entrepreneur assess
the viability and sustainability of
the idea, and then helping them get
their business launched. Incubators
often provide active entrepreneurs with a
place where they can accelerate the growth of
their existing enterprises.

"The Brenau University Idea Development Center ('IDC')
adds two critical stages to the Manufacturing Development Center
concept, by (1) offering eligible students space where they can develop their ideas under the mentorship and guidance of professors,

THE GATEWAY TO INNOVATION AND INCUBATION

experienced entrepreneurs, and the Small Business Development Center; and (2) by helping the students plant the initial seeds that lead to their first commercial successes.

"In effect, the IDC becomes the gateway to innovation and incubation – preparing candidate entrepreneurs for the acceleration stage found in the best incubators.

"Being sponsored and supported by a University is a logical step – but only in so far as the University helps the entrepreneur through the critical transformation step from idea to incubation, and sustainability. The IDC plays a critical role by offering students with an idea or rudimentary business plan flesh out their concepts through a combination of formal education, mentorship, and small business development that enables participants to validate their ideas, establish their businesses, and secure their first sources of funding and/or revenue prior to making the transition to incubation. The partnership between Brenau, Lanier Tech's Manufacturing Development Center (MDC), Georgia Tech Enterprise Innovation Institute, the University of Georgia Small Business Development Center, and experienced business professionals helps nurture burgeoning entrepreneurs at the initial stage in their development. This helps reduce risks of failure while encouraging the next generation of entrepreneurs."

Sheri Hooper

CHAPTER FIVE

INK: Imagining a New "Box"

❧

"This is what a school should look like!"
—BOB ORMSBY, RETIRED PRESIDENT
LOCKHEED AIRCRAFT CORPORATION, ON HIS FIRST VISIT TO INK

Learning does not always take place in the classroom, of course, and few people understand that better than Sheri Hooper. In August 2002, Sheri opened the Interactive Neighborhood for Kids (INK), an extraordinary museum venue that offers children a hands-on learning environment that replicates on a small scale the broader community that exists in Gainesville, Georgia. INK's success can be measured by its number of visitors (approximately 50,000 annually), but its true measure has more to do with the growth and enrichment of children and adults in the North Georgia community. Housed at Featherbone Communiversity since June 2006, INK today has become an integral part of Gainesville's educational system and a favorite learning destination for school, daycare and church groups, as well as families and tourists.

Inside INK are party rooms, arts and crafts areas, and a stage for viewing puppet shows, storytelling or dramas, but the heart of the museum is the "town" beyond that. A stroll down INK's Main Street takes visitors past miniature versions of just about every business or public service destination typically found in the community. Children can visit a grocery store, bank, post office, doctor's office, or library, and discover what it's like to actually be a grocer, a bank teller, a postal clerk, a doctor, or a librarian. Further down the street, they can sit inside the cab of a real fire truck or the cockpit of an airplane and imagine themselves to be a firefighter or pilot. The idea is to give them an opportunity to experience everyday life in the community and discover their own particular interests and aspirations.

"Every children's museum is unique to its own community," Sheri explains. "At INK, we focus on role playing in different careers. It allows the kids to go outside the classroom and their families and see themselves being anybody they want to be, if they work hard at it. It's interesting to see how children tend to focus on one area or another. For example, a child will sit in the airplane the whole time he's here, while others are drawn to entirely different areas. Hopefully, they can find a love or passion, and maybe become masters of teaching themselves when they grow up."

INK frequently invites professionals from the community to participate in Career Day events so children can

meet the people who are already working members of the community. Sheri sees it as an opportunity for children to ask questions that they might not otherwise feel comfortable posing in the real community settings.

"We had an attorney here recently," says Sheri, "who was explaining the legal system to a group of kids, when one of

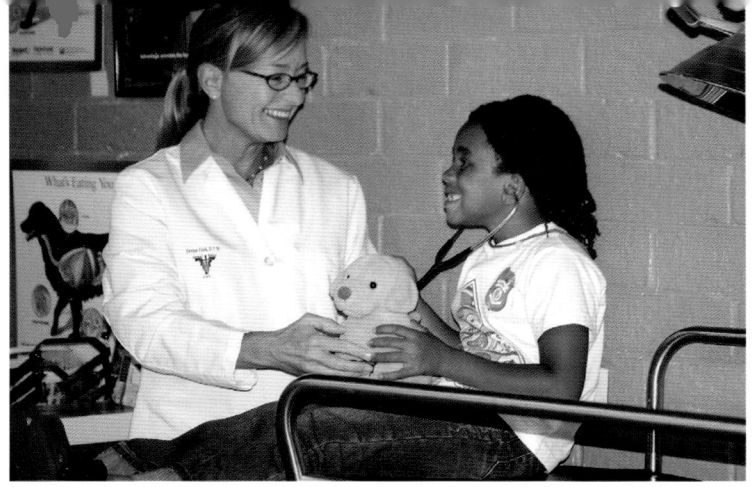

them raised his hand and asked what the food was like in jail. That's the kind of environment we want to encourage, one that lends itself to kids being comfortable enough to ask anything. I've learned a lot myself, and see professionals in a new light from those Career Day events."

Like other children's museums, INK features exhibits designed to entertain while they educate, but it is distinctive in its de-emphasis on high-tech bells and whistles. The exhibits are creative and colorful, but there are few video screens or loud noises and flashing lights. The atmosphere is less akin to the contemporary "edu-tainment" style museums and more along the lines of an "Imaginarium," a term that Sheri agrees best describes INK.

"We're trying to teach the kids that it's about being realistic," Sheri explains. "This is not a Disneyland kind of atmosphere. That's not us, and you can find the high-tech stuff at other museums. What we've found is that parents come back saying they feel more comfortable here. It's a place that encourages kids to use their imagination."

Sheri Hooper first got her inspiration for INK on a visit to a children's museum in San Antonio, Texas. Prior to that, she was a stay-at-home mom with an art background and a love for children, but no clear direction for her life's work.

"When I saw that museum in San Antonio, my jaw dropped," she recalls. "I knew instantly that this is what I wanted to do. The exhibits there included things like a trolley and a life-sized cow. My son Tyler was with me, and at the time he was about five years old. I watched him as he interacted with the exhibits, touching things, exploring, sitting in the trolley. He just came alive. As INK has come together, Tyler has been my little consultant. He likes to say that INK wouldn't be here if it wasn't for him."

In essence, Sheri Hooper's story epitomizes what communiversity is all about. The story could be described as passion and patience followed by the courage to act and follow through, all in the context of serving the needs of the community. It began when she and other moms gathered on a regular basis for Bible study and fellowship, and they decided to develop playgroups for their young children. Sheri developed a passion for helping those children learn through exploration and using their imaginations, the same process that she believes was so important to her own learning experience.

"Not everyone learns in the same way," she explains. "Some children are better with direction, and some learn better if you don't give them direction. It took me until I was in high school to finally be able to create a paragraph, and it was frustrating. I am more of an explorer, a doer, and Tyler is the same way. I finally had a teacher who taught outside the box, and that's when I really began to enjoy learning."

To put that concept into practice, Sheri transformed her basement into a hands-on learning environment for the playgroups that came with their mothers for regular visits. She subdivided the space into different areas for reading, arts and crafts, or watching videos. But it wasn't until that trip to San Antonio that Sheri got the idea for a community-wide children's museum. And once she was "captured" by the vision, the vision wouldn't let go. She lay awake at night for months, praying for guidance and thinking about the possibilities. The challenges were significant, and she knew that success could only come with help from others in the community. With support and encouragement from her Sunday School class, she began to put feet on her vision.

"Our first location in 2002 was on the second floor of the old First Methodist Church building, which was owned by the Arts Council," Sheri recalls. "A number of people came forward and volunteered to help create and build out the space. We had a party room, a doctor's office, a store, and several other exhibits. People kept donating materials and bringing items in. It just kept growing until after about nine months we ran out of space."

Growth also meant that INK would require more attention to organization and administrative issues. It meant more responsibility, and as a non-profit, it also meant more accountability. But Sheri did it right. She aligned herself with other professional organizations and individuals who encouraged and advised her through the early stages of development. She secured a strong group of community-minded people to serve on staff and on her board of directors. They have kept her grounded without diminishing her passion and creativity.

"I wanted to do it right," Sheri explains. "I was naive at first and didn't do everything perfectly right. But I knew I wanted it to be non-profit because I wanted everything to go back into the organization, back to the kids. The board has been great. They have helped me with raising funds, and it was one of them who introduced me to Gus and Featherbone Communiversity."

Today, in its newer location at Featherbone Communiversity, INK continues to grow through donations and support from the community at large. And much of the day-to-day work is still conducted with the help of volunteers. Sheri works with the volunteers to determine what their talents are and how they can best fit into the work at INK.

"I believe it's better to talk and listen to people and see where they can fit, rather than trying to make the person fit the job," Sheri says. "If they flow into that area naturally, then they are more likely to feel fulfilled. Volunteers come to us and want to help because they are appreciated, they feel wanted, and they feel that they belong. That's what a neighborhood is, a place where people can feel wanted and feel they belong."

INK has indeed been a community-wide endeavor. The support from businesses, churches, individuals and the media has been exceptional. People continue to volunteer and make donations, businesses continue to sponsor, and professionals continue to offer their time and resources to help build and enhance the hands-on learning environment at INK.

"Once the public figured out the concept," Sheri says, "it has gone over extremely well, and everyone has been very supportive. We're still pinching pennies and don't have a lot of money for marketing, but word of mouth has been exceptional. I believe INK is a good example of how communities work. Community means people reaching out to others, knowing who your neighbors are and having friends who you can call and know that if you need them, they will be there. It's sharing ideas and working together to make things happen...things that make the community better as a whole.

"We are a giving and sharing community here in

Gainesville. There's a spirit of working together here as opposed to people working in their own directions. It's people working in partnerships that will take us so much farther than doing our own things in our own time and our own way."

As part of Featherbone Communiversity, INK embodies one part of the philosophy that makes communiversity effective, and that's the concept of intergenerational learning. It's no surprise that teachers, parents, and other adults find INK to be as fascinating and enjoyable as the children who visit. In a building that for so many years was all about manufacturing clothing for children, it's even more fulfilling to know that Featherbone Communiversity still serves the needs of children while it provides learning opportunities for older generations.

Sheri's selfless spirit has drawn others to her work and gained her a number of awards and recognition from service organizations and businesses in the area. Her vision for INK has far surpassed her original thinking, but her approach has not changed. She still has a clear purpose in providing learning opportunities for the community. Truly a servant at heart, her deep desire is to encourage others—children and adults—to imagine, to connect, and to follow their dreams.

"I want to see more people discovering what they want to do, or who they want to be, or what they are passionate about. And when they do, I hope they are willing to step forward and make the leap."

INTERACTIVE NEIGHBORHOOD FOR KIDS

JAN GILMER
Guest Services
Coordinator

*T*alk to Jan Gilmer about her four grand-children, her two great-grandchildren, or the tens of thousands of kids who come through INK's doors every year, and her face lights up. She loves children, and she especially enjoys helping them grow and learn during their vis-its to the children's museum where she serves as the Guest Services Coordinator. But that genuine love behind her warm smile is only half of what makes her the ideal person for her job at INK. Jan, who first came to INK as a volunteer in its early days, brought administrative skills that quickly became an invaluable asset to the organization—so much so that INK's director asked her to come on board as a permanent staff member.

After serving as a stay-at-home mom in her early adult years, Jan later embarked on a career that included a broad and diverse work experience. She attended technical school, worked sev-eral years in aerospace manufacturing, and for five years with engineers at TriNova in Toccoa, Georgia. During those years, she honed her administrative skills before steering her career path in another direction. She became a certified nursing assistant and for many years was a caretaker in assisted living environments. It's that combination of business skills and caretaking that makes Jan's arrival at INK seem an unusually fortunate match. She is the perfect host. Ask anyone who visits INK and they will quickly tell you that to be greeted and received by Jan Gilmer is indeed an experience that makes them feel loved.

"I do have administrative skills that are important here at INK," says Jan, whose responsibilities include managing money and record keeping, " but as Guest Services Coordinator I try to make people feel comfortable, welcomed and appreciated. I'm a nurturer who wants people who come here to feel loved and cared for."

Jan believes that INK's location at Featherbone Communiversity is another confirmation that she is supposed to be there. She has fond memories of standing in line to buy baby clothes at Warren Featherbone's outlet store when it operated in the same location.

"People come into INK and ask if this is where they used to make baby clothes," she says. "I tell them 'yes' and that having a children's learning museum here now is the height of recycling."

INK SUPPORTERS...

DOUG HANSON
Dedicated Grandfather

To say that Doug Hanson takes his role as a grandfather seriously is an understatement. After 40 successful years in sales and marketing with DuPont, Doug Hanson retired early. He wanted to spend more time with his six grandchildren.

To four of those six grandchildren, Doug was their only grandfather. Due to circumstances in his own family growing up, there was no grandparent, and as a result he is very intentional in everything he does as a grandfather. He says grandparenting is like getting a second chance at parenting, a "do-over with wisdom."

Doug met Sheri Hooper, INK's founder, as she was refining her dream for the children's learning museum. He remembers her early days of at-home education, when day trips for learning were the rewards. Going to INK is a big deal for the Hanson family. During their visits, they take photos and compile scrapbooks. Doug recently carried one of those scrapbooks to Egar, Hungary, one of Gainesville's two sister-cities. (The other is Izunokuni, Shizuoka Prefecture, Japan.).

"Preparing kids for many eventualities," says Doug, describing INK. "This includes play, real-world careers, and IMAGINATION!"

Doug believes INK is a truly unique resource for the family because:

1. It's local to our area.
2. It's a very friendly place in a campus-like atmosphere.
3. It's grandparent-friendly (one level with no steps), and has large restrooms for diaper changing.
4. The exhibits are always new and refreshing.
5. Through self-directed play, children learn independence. They also learn about people who serve our society such as firemen, policemen, doctors and others.
6. INK is also educational for adults. Numerous workshops of interest to adults are regularly held there including painting, ballet, crafts, and careers of all types, taught by real-life practitioners.

In summary, Doug describes what INK provides as seen through the eyes of a granddad: "Given the opportunity to be a granddad is one of the greatest gifts and challenges in life, and developing resources of fun and learning are key to being an intentional grandfather. INK supplies all the ingredients to meet these opportunities: a strong learning environment in a compact, friendly location that augments with fun and purpose what is taught and experienced in the home. INK is always a hit and a constant surprise."

PHILLIPPA LEWIS MOSS
INK Board Chair and Mother

Phillippa Lewis Moss is busy! She is director of the Gainesville/Hall County Community Service Center, Chair of the Board of INK, and mom of six-year-old Na'im. As a parent, Phillippa bought most of her baby clothes over the years from Warren Featherbone in the same location that is now known as INK. As a shopper, she felt "at home" at Warren Featherbone. People were organic (real), hype was absent, and it was a comfortable place to be. So it is today at INK, she says, adding that the same spirit prevails in a different form.

Phillippa has also seen tremendous growth at INK. Attendance has grown to more than 4,000 visitors per month and, in 2008, *Atlanta Parent Magazine* named INK Number 1 in the "10 Timeless Treasures" of Georgia. By observing her son Na'im and others, she believes she knows why:

1. INK is the right size. It is built for kids with the right height and level of messaging. It is very understandable to a child without being superficial or irrelevant. INK truly becomes a child's second home.

2. Children are treated as guests and welcomed there by the INK staff.

3. Because they are made to feel at home, children feel protective of the learning museum and become hosts themselves. Phillippa feels this social interaction is one of the most important benefits of a child's visit to INK.

4. INK is "hands-on" and provides important physical activity from the jungle gym to the fire truck and trains.

5. INK offers practical help for parents too. As an example, Na'im dreads going to the dentist. To prepare for the real visit, Phillippa takes Na'im to the dentist office at INK where they role-play "going to the dentist," which she says helps a lot.

6. INK is never boring. Phillippa says her son could play all day at INK, twenty days out of the month! The reason is his ever-expanding imagination and the important social interaction with other kids.

To sum up the magic at INK, Phillippa says, "In an age when we are trying to protect children against negative forces (images, language, and so forth), INK offers a sanctuary for young souls. In this place, they grow physically, intellectually and spiritually."

Elaine Pulliam
First Grade Teacher

Elaine Pulliam has been involved as a volunteer with INK since its inception eight years ago when the children's learning museum was located in the church building. She has been bringing her son Grant to INK since he was nine months old. Elaine is now a first grade teacher at Sugar Hill Elementary School in Hall County, Georgia. For the past six years she has brought the entire first grade from her school to visit INK. Like many schools in Georgia which also schedule field trips to INK, Sugar Hill Elementary will bring approximately 150-170 students who will first discover INK in this way.

Elaine explains to her students that INK is a very unusual museum. Most museums encourage students to "look but don't touch." At INK, however, they can "look and touch." She feels that INK broadens horizons for children and provides experiences that might not be possible otherwise, especially in challenging economic times. She tells us that in visiting the exhibits and "trying on" the careers represented children learn:

1. To serve with courtesy (50's café, beauty shop)
2. To show compassion to animals (pet clinic)
3. To learn what business is all about (grocery store, bank)
4. To care for each other (doctor's and dentist's office, clinic, North Georgia Health System's "Buddy" exhibit). On entering the "dentist's office," one of Elaine's students exclaimed, "I'm going to be a dentist!"
5. To care for society (fire truck, sheriff's car)
6. To be creative in the arts (painting, pottery, theater)
7. To transport our nation (trains, Grandpappy Airlines)
8. To clean up! INK is spotless and Elaine's last activity for her students is to clean up when the visit is ending to have it ready for the next visitor.

When Elaine Pulliam comes to INK she is, in a way, coming home. As the daughter of Jerry and Jackie Deal, you could say Elaine grew up in Warren Featherbone. Her mother, Jackie Deal, was the beloved credit manager for Warren Featherbone for twenty years. Elaine remembers as a little girl being proud that something so large yet so helpful for children existed in Gainesville. And then there were all those baby clothes for her dolls! For Elaine, Warren Featherbone was always about helping children and their families. Through INK it still is, but in a new and exciting way.

Dr. Ed Schrader

CHAPTER SIX

Brenau University: A Heritage of Innovation

⤸

D r. Ed Schrader loves rocks, and not just a little bit. He considers rocks and the study of geology as one of his lifelong passions. And he describes passion as that thing that "absolutely gives you chills when you do it... and would keep you sleepless at night as you anticipate doing it the next morning." As president of Brenau University in Gainesville, Georgia, Dr. Schrader encourages his students to pursue their passions, not just for their own edification but because it can literally change the world.

"I know you have passion," Dr. Schrader recently said to a graduating class. "I have seen it in your life and your accomplishments. I have seen it in your service to others. Use your excitement to change the world."

Dr. Schrader's early interest in geology led to a Ph.D. from Duke University and recognition as a much-published geochemical researcher. With his education and knowledge, as well as his astute business sense and leadership skills, he certainly could have gone far in his industry. In the late 1980s, on his way to the top of his field, Dr. Schrader realized that getting there would require too much time away from his family, more than he wanted to sacrifice. Besides that, he felt unfulfilled, as if there was something else he was supposed to do, something that would have a more meaningful impact and leave a lasting legacy. He turned to education, and began a career in pursuit of a growing passion in his life—helping others learn through higher education. Admittedly good at business and finance, he realized he could bring those skills to bear in a field where he could help colleges and universities shape their legacies. He made a conscious shift in his career path, and since then higher education has been the beneficiary.

In January 2005, Dr. Schrader became the ninth president of Brenau University, which was founded in 1878. Among those nine leaders was Dr. H.J. Pearce, who served the college from 1893 until 1943. Dr. Pearce was visionary and in 1928 established Brenau Academy which provided college preparation for young women in grades 9-12. It was also Dr. Pearce who wrote "The Brenau Ideal" that continues to define Brenau's spirit:

· *To find satisfaction in being rather than in seeming;*
· *To find joy in doing rather than in dreaming;*

- *To be prepared for service thereby earning the right to be served;*
- *To be pure in heart, vigorous in mind, discreet in action;*
- *To love deeply, fear nothing, hate never;*
- *To enjoy that freedom that comes from knowledge of the "Truth";*
- *To be modestly conscious of the limitations of human knowledge and serenely confident of the limitless reaches of human endeavor — this is the ideal of Brenau.*

Like his predecessor, Dr. Schrader's vision for Brenau University is about finding "joy in doing" and preparing students for life in their communities that goes beyond the ordinary. He has made his mark in education by looking beyond the traditions of the past and the "limitations of human knowledge." Under his leadership, Brenau University is embracing present-day innovative learning tools and technologies, and is moving forward boldly into the future with confidence in "the limitless reaches of human endeavor." The university has recently redefined and expanded its program with a stated mission to become by the year 2025 a nationally recognized and regionally preferred doctoral institution "unique in its educational process."

"*Brenau 2025*" is the university's action plan which has been designed to create innovative ways to educate that will prepare students to live extraordinary lives.

Brenau's forward-thinking approach to learning is not new with Dr. Schrader; his willingness to break the mold is a part of the university's heritage. Originally named the Georgia Baptist Female Seminary, the school changed its name in 1900 to Brenau College to better reflect its mission and its distinctions from other schools of that era.

"Brenau was founded at a time when many secondary schools for women were just finishing schools where students were primed for finding a good marriage partner," explains Dr. Schrader. "But the trustees at Brenau were genuinely interested in the intellectual and professional value of women, as well as their moral and spiritual character. One of the historical elements of this university has been its stance for social equity. Our new mission statement today continues that idea."

During the latter half of the 20th century, single-gender schools declined significantly, primarily because of competition and financial stresses. In the 1960s, there were nearly 400 women's colleges in the U.S., but today the number is down to about 55. Dr. Schrader points to past leadership and innovative approaches to learning for Brenau's continued success in recent times.

"In the 1970s, the trustees recognized that there was

a growing need for additional education among adults already in the workplace," says Dr. Schrader, "and Brenau began offering co-ed evening and weekend college courses, which added another revenue stream. By the 1980s, the evening and weekend enrollment exceeded the women's college. Then, in the late 1990s, Brenau leadership recognized the trend toward online programs and added that third alternative, which is doing well."

Today, Brenau University has an overall enrollment of approximately 2,760, with 900 in the women's college, 1,500 in the co-ed evening and weekend program, 60 at Brenau Academy (college preparatory high school) and more than 300 in the online college. The university expects significant growth in the online program and overall expects to double enrollment to 5,000 within ten years.

"I believe Brenau has survived through the years because we had academic integrity, and we were willing to adapt and embrace those new avenues for learning," explains Dr. Schrader. "Part of that adaptive facet is the result of having trustees who are not so bound by traditions that they won't listen to criticism and innovative ideas about education."

Brenau's trustees are active in the community but they are not predominantly Brenau alumnae, which has likely helped them make "big picture" decisions that benefited the university without feeling they were anchored to a tradition or approach that was no longer viable. Interestingly, the school has historically hired presidents who were not bound by heritage, and Dr. Schrader echoes the wisdom of that approach when he says, "Our job is to preserve the heritage without letting it cause the demise of the school."

"At the same time," he adds, "it's important to note that Brenau's trustees have a great affection and commitment to the school and, because they are mostly from the area, they see the historical importance of having the university here in this community. People that are closely involved with Brenau University understand its connection to the community of Gainesville. This university supplies the majority of nurses in this area, the occupational therapists, and the educators. Brenau generates many of the cultural events in the community, and we have two stages that are booked 365 days a year either in cultural events or performances that are practicing or happening."

For more than a century and a quarter, Brenau has been a treasure to the northeast Georgia region, and no less so today. Brenau's cultural and economic impact on the community is significant. The university's budget was $40 million for 2008, but its overall economic impact is estimated to be about $80 million for the Gainesville community. Much of that consists of money flowing into the local economy from outside the community for tuition, gas, health services, clothing, and such.

Brenau University's heritage of innovative learning helps to explain in part why the school's leadership enthusiastically embraced the concept of community learning as represented by Featherbone Communiversity. In 2006, needing to relocate Brenau's growing school of nursing, university leaders met with Featherbone Communiversity and agreed to transform 37,000 square feet of former manufacturing space into what has now become the Brenau East Campus. In August 2007, the first classes were held there and students and faculty are now learning in a dynamic, state-of-the-art facility that includes media-friendly classrooms, computer labs, healthcare simulation rooms, and a remarkable simulator patient named iStan, who isn't human but looks and acts like one. Brenau also has created a complex at the new location for their dance and theatre schools. Dr. Schrader believes moving to Featherbone Communiversity was a great fit.

"I think of communiversity as a Disneyland of the mind, like Epcot, where people actually pay to go into a place and learn," says Dr. Schrader. "What's important is exposure of individuals to all aspects of human knowledge and natural truths throughout their lives. And communiversity is an opportunity for that to happen."

Included in the goals of Brenau's action plan is an evolutionary learning experience called "Portals of Learning," which the university describes as a "new and richer means of understanding and relating to our world." The idea is to take students beyond traditional learning and provide them with "doorways" to the international community, a world that has become a "fast-paced, information-centric, scientifically demanding, and culturally diverse global society." Brenau's programs encourage students to reach beyond their comfort zones and pursue the extraordinary, so they will be prepared to meet life's challenges with a "sense of curiosity rather than fear, of innovation rather than acceptance."

Brenau University's presence at Featherbone Communiversity has already proven to be beneficial. Collaboration with others located there began immediately.

"Our nurses learning pediatrics volunteer at INK," says Dr. Keeta Wilborn, who directs the Department of Nursing at Brenau, "They have to learn about growth and development, and at INK they can watch the kids interact and learn what is normal before learning what's not. They help with kids of all ages, preschool and up. They have become a part of what's going on there."

> *"...it's not just the building that makes communiversity work. It's the idea of people of all ages in the community learning together."*
>
> — Gus Whalen

For nurses learning pediatrics, involvement next

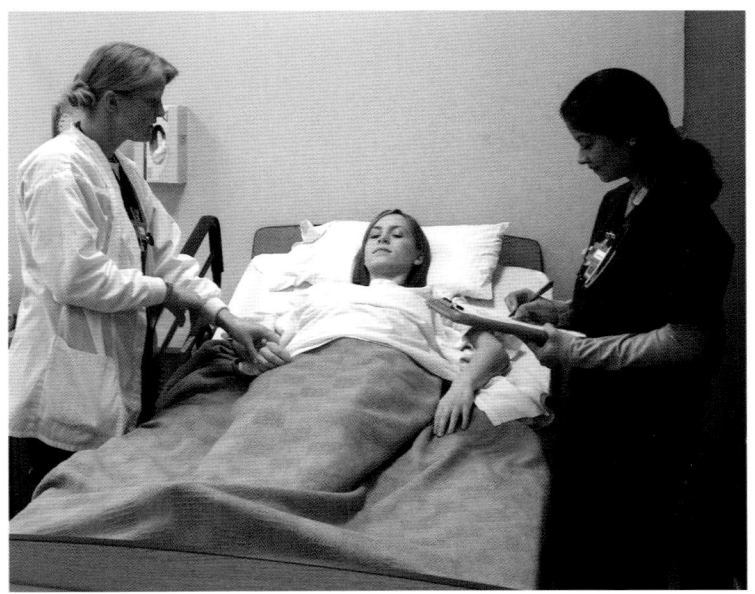

Brenau nursing students "in action."

door at INK was almost a given, but the collaboration between Brenau's Department of Nursing and Lanier Tech's Manufacturing Development Center was an unexpected surprise. Working together, they are developing new technologies for patient care including a device for helping turn patients. This device will go a long way toward alleviating a growing problem for nurses: back injuries.

"The collaboration has been great," says Dr. Wilborn, "and being here has enabled the nursing school to go outside the campus and interact with the broader community. The auditorium is used for community health programs, such as the Southside Community Fair, which brings in a lot of healthcare professionals to provide blood screening and other health testing. We also host a Career Day for students in Health and Science, and invite different employers to come and present."

The auditorium at Brenau University has already become a favorite location for cultural events, conferences, and other community functions. On tap for the future are two events that represent the kind of innovative and forward looking learning opportunities that define what communiversity is all about. The first will be *Masters in Teaching ...Life Changers at Work.* The purpose of this conference is to better understand the characteristics of our very best and life-changing teachers, to affirm them, and to encourage others like them to enter the field of teaching. The second event will occur on **Earth Day 2009** and will be co-sponsored by Brenau University, the Elachee Nature Center, and several local educational institutions and churches. The Earth Day initiative in our community began with Frank Armstrong, local attorney and past president of Elachee. The keynote speaker for 2009 will be Janisse Ray, an award-winning Georgia author and environmental activist, whose presentation will be broadcast simultaneously to area schools.

So when in your life does learning stop? At Featherbone

Communiversity it never does. That's why Brenau University, an institute of higher learning whose presence has always permeated the community, has found a home there. But it's not just the building that makes communiversity work. It's the idea of people of all ages in the community learning together.

"Communiversity is not tied to the building," Dr. Schrader summarizes. "There might be participants who are not even in the facility. The idea is to bring people together to learn collaboratively and be organically related. Communiversity is part of an engaging relationship, as opposed to an exclusive one. At Brenau, we are a private school that reaches out to the whole community. We are a mosaic of non-profit entities held in trust for the public good. At Featherbone Communiversity, the coming together for mutually beneficial, life-long learning is the ultimate goal as I see it."

How are you continuing to learn? College? Post-college? Or, if you've been out of school for many years, how can you join others in learning in your community? Is there a spirit of communiversity alive where you live? Hopefully so, but if not, maybe it's time to begin.

WELCOME TO
GAINESVILLE/
HALL COUNTY, GA

BRENAU UNIVERSITY EAST
INK
LANIER TECHNICAL COLLEGE
GEORGIA TECH
THE UNIV OF GEORGIA-SBDC

The lighting of the Featherbone Communiversity sign in January, 2008.

CHAPTER SEVEN

Featherbone Communiversity
From the Educator's Perspective

*eatherbone Communiversity was dedicated on October 18, 2007, and today is guided by the collaborative efforts of six educational institutions. They are Brenau

University, Gainesville City Schools, Gainesville State College, Hall County Schools, Interactive Neighborhood for Kids (INK), and Lanier Technical College (in cooperation with Georgia Tech and the University of Georgia). We are becoming the learning community that learns together.

The following individuals, all educational leaders and among the founding trustees of Featherbone Communiversity, represent public and private education. Here they share their insights and discoveries as we embark on this journey called communiversity.

Featherbone Communiversity as a Model

By Dr. Martha T. Nesbitt

DR. NESBITT IS PRESIDENT OF GAINESVILLE STATE COLLEGE WHICH OPERATES ON TWO CAMPUSES WITH AN ENROLLMENT OF APPROXIMATELY 8,500.

Education is critical to the social, political and economic strength of a community. In this regard, everyone knows the importance of good schools and access to quality higher education. In addition to traditional education, there has been increased emphasis in the past few decades on lifelong-learning. Economic globalization and rapidly changing technology have been the primary catalysts behind this movement. It also stems, however, from the desire for self-fulfillment among an older population who may have "retired" from their careers but seek to continue learning and contributing to society.

In addition to the need to improve both formal and informal education, there needs to be connections within a community if it is to thrive. Communiversity is a mechanism to bring these three elements together in a unique way.

Featherbone Communiversity in Gainesville, Georgia, is creating a model that brings a community together and provides opportunities for enhancing education and connectivity. In other words, it promotes community learning. It developed during a time when the Gainesville/Hall County community was engaged in a visioning process. Participants from all areas of the county engaged in focus groups to develop a plan of what they want our community to look like in the year 2030. The result was Vision 2030, and one of its major goals is to raise the educational level in the community. It also seeks to connect different ethnic groups to create common goals.

Featherbone Communiversity is one of the earliest manifestations of Vision 2030 and epitomizes the spirit of the plan. Its uniqueness lies in bringing together programs and creating a synergy that enhances their success. It also makes a statement that the Gainesville community recognizes the importance of education and connections.

One man's vision inspired the community to take the concept and develop it. Gus Whalen brought together a group of community leaders to share his vision and engage them in the process of moving from concept to fruition. In about two years, Featherbone Communiversity attracted important programs and became a bustling center of activity. The development is a dynamic process, and Featherbone Communiversity will likely look very different in ten to fifteen years. It will certainly have new components as people continue to dream and seek ways to strengthen the community.

When communities come together to learn, they establish bonds and common goals. People learn more about their community and discover needs and challenges that may not be part of their everyday life. They see the importance of holistically approaching issues that need attention, and understand the interdependence necessary for a healthy community. Community learning through Featherbone Communiversity can take the form of traditional classes, political and social forums, focus groups that come together to discuss specific issues, and programs that celebrate both community successes and individuals, such as model teachers, who influence our children in so many positive ways. Communiversity should be seen as a gathering place that brings together many different organizations and agencies in the community to learn and work together.

As a college president, I know that many of our students will have jobs that don't even exist today. So our purpose is to provide them with a solid educational foundation and to prepare them to continue learning, to be creative and to be flexible. Creativity will be critical to their futures. In like fashion, a dynamic Communiversity will evolve with continuing vision, creativity and tenacity by those who see the tremendous benefits to our community.

While not having a crystal ball to see specific programs of the future, I see Featherbone Communiversity collaborating with the public schools to provide supplemental instruction, with colleges and universities in providing special programs, with business and industry to promote economic development, with government to promote participation in political processes, with environmental groups to promote a healthy environment and sustainability, and with social service agencies to better serve those with special needs.

The development of Featherbone Communiversity brings to mind the parable of the mustard seed "that someone took and sowed in his field; it is the smallest of all seeds, but when it has grown it is the greatest of shrubs and becomes a tree, so that the birds of the air come and make nests in its branches." As Featherbone Communiversity continues its evolution, it can become the nest for many parts of this community as it seeks to fulfill its vision. It will also continue to enhance a sense of community, promote a strong synergy, and support efforts that enhance its overall health. The future is ours to create, and we will need people to dream large.

What is Communiversity and Why is it Relevant?

By Dr. Ed L. Schrader

DR. SCHRADER IS PRESIDENT OF BRENAU UNIVERSITY, WHICH OPERATES FOUR CAMPUSES WITH A TOTAL ENROLLMENT OF APPROXIMATELY 2,760 STUDENTS.

In my Utopian society, the local community of all citizens—all ages—share collectively in organized groups, or spontaneously, their personal knowledge and experience. Augmenting more formal education, this pooling of knowledge, heightened by the experiences of life, gives birth to a mutual community characteristic: wisdom. Unfortunately, this spontaneous collaboration very rarely occurs as we are left to our own devices of surviving life in the 21st century. We have to be intentional, with a steady but soft influence in directing events and groups toward each other. The coming together for mutually beneficial, life-long learning is the ultimate goal of Communiversity as I see it. A community with shared wisdom would lift the quality of living and enjoying life for all. But it will not come about by happenstance. It must be intentional.

I am certain that one model cannot be universal. It is obvious that any community will have multiple and diverse needs to continue learning, outside and beyond classrooms and structure. But since there already are many "continuing education" and government-sponsored programs targeting specific social objectives, why do we need yet another "trendy" new name and program to dilute the thin public (and private) support for education? I suppose that if you do not have a firm grasp of the potential for Communiversity and the "learning/wisdom" it can promulgate, then that question will be all you need to make you stop reading this note and stop you from considering that potential.

To me, Communiversity is a way for generally independent and unrelated groups to work together toward various programs or projects leading to community learning. Community learning starts when these disparate and mostly unrelated groups begin to collaborate on a project. Although the project goal may be a particular learning event or opportunity, the process of learning has already begun when the separate groups are united in concept and cooperation. We have then learned to synergize our efforts and create an intellectual or artistic whole that is greater than the sum of the parts. Sounds trite and cliché, but we usually do not think to collaborate due to turf protection, limited time set aside to focus on collaboration, and the deadly pursuit of the day to day needs of our own organizations. So, the first learning is by the collaborating organizations themselves.

Next, many opportunities exist for a community to share in learning experiences that do not neatly fall into the jurisdiction of a single group or organization. Take Earth Day. No one group has the public or private "rights" to that special day of observation and nobody is really chastised by the "bosses" if he or she does not do anything to observe Earth Day. Earth Day is a perfect focus for the community of educational groups to collaborate in bringing an educational experience to the larger community they all serve. Other scenarios for Communiversity-based learning could include artistic performances; gallery exhibitions rising from the collective works or efforts of multiple members from several separate groups, institutions, or organizations; co-hosting a visiting special speaker or teacher; community organization into service-learning projects; serving as a venue(s) for community "listening" by planning groups or political figures, to name a few.

Right now we are concentrating on activities more or less centered on a physical place, the Featherbone Communiversity building. However, for useful survival beyond the tenure of the founding forces, the idea of Communiversity must become accepted as a relevant and useful contributor to the betterment of life for folks living in and around its host community. Just as United Way has become inculcated in local societies, a Communiversity must be a thread in the fabric of life without which that fabric as we know it becomes weaker and perhaps unravels.

What of the future? Cannot a Communiversity be a communications hub for public use and beneficial access? With the advent of podcasts, internet communications, and local area cable and computer networks, a Communiversity can distribute all manner of information and just plain fun to its community. Then, perhaps, the community enlarges and becomes global as electronic media carries the message and programs to any who would care to hear, learn or participate! What a wonderful outcome! Could we generate a global community with a shared, global pool of wisdom?

Could a Communiversity serve as catalyst for multiple groups to contribute intellectual capital and talent for scientific, social, or financial research? Certainly. All that is necessary is the collaborative will and intentionality to do so. The research would be community based and shared in ownership by all participating entities. Many smaller colleges and technical institutions have talented staff but in numbers too small to support significant research. A collection of professionals from several such small institutions could create a group faculty rivaling those of major institutions.

Communiversity can take you where your interest lies. One model is not universally applicable. If we are focused, committed, and intentional then these collaborative benefits are available to all! I look forward to your contribution to the wisdom pool!

The Concept of Communiversity and its Potential to Shape Schools

By Will Schofield

WILL SCHOFIELD IS
SUPERINTENDENT OF HALL
COUNTY SCHOOLS, WHICH
INCLUDES 34 ELEMENTARY,
MIDDLE AND HIGH SCHOOLS,
AND AN ENROLLMENT OF
NEARLY 26,000.

There is an image to which almost all of us can relate – 800-square-foot linoleum-floored rooms lined with little desks; relatively structured surroundings; approximately 6 hours of activity between 8 a.m. and 3 p.m., all being directed by a single teacher of 15 to 30 young learners. In designing the concept of the American school, John Dewey and his counterparts envisioned an institution that would develop citizens, instill a loyalty for country, and demonstrate beyond question an egalitarian belief in the worth of all people, regardless of race, gender, national origin or disability. I would argue that, in spite of current popular rhetoric, the American School Experience has been a resounding success in accomplishing these tasks.

On a personal level, your school memories may conjure up visions of Mrs. Owens, Coach Thompson, or your first date. Mine contains an olfactory memory so strong that I can still smell the boxed potatoes and yeast rolls prepared in the basement cafeteria of a Wisconsin elementary school. The point is, most of our generation's rich recollections of school memories involve affective and personal musings rather than seismic changes in the way we thought or learned.

The American concept of school is one that has changed very little over the past 100 years. 11/9 (1989), not to be confused with 9/11, marked the beginning of a series of world events our grandparents could have never imagined. The prophetic words of former President Ronald Reagan came to fruition as the Berlin Wall collapsed and Eastern Europe entered the world economic scene. The succeeding decade witnessed India and China emerging from a Third World stupor with their meteoric birth rates and a steely determination to lead the world in manufacturing and knowledge work. Our own nation, meanwhile, held fast to the path that had served us well in another era.

As Gus noted earlier, someone once said, "If the

horse is dead, dismount." I would argue that while our current school structure is not dead, it is ill and in need of change. Our own Communiversity has the potential to help Hall County modernize our concept of schooling to meet the demands of a changing world. The 21st-century conceptual age will ask our children to learn and work in unprecedented ways. Learning must transform into a dynamic, individualized, relevant process that taps into the vast knowledge resources of our entire community.

The concept of teaching must be redefined to include any process that facilitates the development of another's skills, beliefs, or abilities. Grandparents, CEO's, factory workers, virtual resources, and community assets of all kinds must be tapped to help boys and girls, moms and dads, even grandparents further develop a voracious appetite for life-long learning and creative thought. The inclusion of virtual programming, ipods, webcasts, and even relevant discussions around kitchen tables will further stretch our ability to structure formal teaching differently. Likewise, our concept of "school" sits ready to evolve.

Too often we associate school with a facility, a red brick building filled with cubicles in which teaching and learning occur. But, not unlike the concept of a church, a school is not really a building. We need to remember that in its purest sense a school should be the loosely coupled resources that facilitate the process of learning. Communiversity will provide a catalyst for the consideration of part-time programming, different methods of learning at home, smorgasbords of virtual learning opportunities; and perhaps, most importantly, it will provide a forum and platform in which our concepts of teaching and learning can be challenged and expanded.

Swimming against the stream of common thought and past experience, the future of schooling is bright. A wise individual once stated, "Only those who can see the invisible can do the impossible." Does Communiversity hold the potential to reshape our schools into institutions that will effectively serve our most valued resource, our boys and girls? It does. It must. It will.

Communiversity is a Vibrant Force

By Dr. Michael D. Moye

DR. MOYE IS PRESIDENT OF LANIER TECHNICAL COLLEGE IN OAKWOOD, GEORGIA, WHICH SERVES NEARLY 30,000 STUDENTS THROUGH LONG-TERM DEGREE AND DIPLOMA PROGRAMS AS WELL AS ECONOMIC DEVELOPMENT AND ADULT LITERACY NON-CREDIT PROGRAMS.

Communiversity can be whatever the community wants it to be. While traditional learning primarily takes place in the classrooms of public and private schools and in colleges, communiversity can be a catalyst that sparks creative educational opportunities that are very "out-of-the-box" in our traditional educational settings. Typically, colleges join with local school systems, with government operated entities (Parks and Recreation) and with local non-profit organizations (Girls and Boys Club, YMCA) to offer a vast array of special interest (non-credit) classes for young and old alike. The limitation that Featherbone Communiversity overcomes is bringing all of these entities to the table to talk about and plan for cooperative educational opportunities that might have been overlooked.

Whatever form communiversity takes, it is still about community learning. Community learning happens when a city, county, or even a region is engaged in moving beyond "status quo". It happens when people recognize that there is much more to life than eat, sleep, and work. Community learning is an important facet in the well-rounded growth of a group of people living together in an area. It identifies what people not only need to learn, but also what they want to learn. All communities are made up of groups of people and entities that have a common interest within the group. Often, the group or entity is willing to share its knowledge or expertise so that others may appreciate what the group holds to be important.

When we have a learning environment that permeates the entire community, we find that lives are greatly enriched by the knowledge that is shared among groups and individuals. A group is often only concerned with its own members or constituency. It does not look beyond its natural boundaries and seek out ways to share a particular body of knowledge with others. A community truly dedicated to learning approaches education and training in a much different fashion. They are heavily engaged in communicating with one another to find out what's available and how it can be delivered to all sectors of the community.

Communiversity also serves as a catalyst for bringing together diverse groups of people, such as people of different age groups, in ways that can benefit the community at large. As people live longer and retire earlier, the need for intergenerational learning comes into view. Intergenerational learning is centered on the needs of both youth and older citizens, but rather than viewing those needs as problems, it sees them as potential resources that can be tapped to provide solutions for both groups. Among both groups are individuals, both young and old, who want to share their wisdom, skills and knowledge. They are a vast resource of abilities and talents, and they offer potential solutions that are in need of a problem to solve.

The future of community learning in our area will be greatly enhanced and expanded by the participants in Featherbone Communiversity. The participating community has a great deal of educational activity already taking place, but Communiversity participants will create potentially new and exciting family-school-community partnerships that will have a positive impact on every corner of the community. In the future, people who value learning can have an opportunity to communicate, to share, to explore thinking and problem solving. They can enrich the fabric of their lives with increased opportunities to participate in a true intergenerational exchange of ideas and information. Far into the future, Featherbone Communiversity will be a vibrant community force having great influence on the educational opportunities found in the city and county.

The University of Cambridge, founded in 1209

CHAPTER EIGHT

A New Loaf

❦

*S*ome say that communiversity may be the next evolution of the university, and that evolution brings us full circle to the local community. This is an interesting point to consider. By way of background, the first higher education institution in medieval Europe was the University of Constantinople, followed by the University of Salerno (9th century), and the first degree-granting universities in Europe were the University of Bologna (1088), the University of Paris (1150), the University of Oxford (1167), and the University of Cambridge (1209). The word university is derived from Latin *universitas magistorem et scholarium*, which means "community of teachers and scholars." The first universities in the United States were Harvard, William and Mary, and Yale, all built during the Colonial period on the plans of Oxford and Cambridge.

In general, universities see themselves as learning centers where all sciences get shared for the good of society. Increasingly, their reach is international and their community is the world. In some sense, many are like large businesses that have become transnational corporations with global brands. In contrast, the current communiversity movement seeks to develop learning communities at the local level from the inside out.

The first Conference on Communiversity was organized by educators and futurists, Gus and Joanne Jaccaci, and held July 2008 at Pineland Farms in New Gloucester, Maine. Twelve communiversities attended, including five being established in Maine in cooperation with Maine's Department of Economic and Community Development. These communiversities vary widely in their form, from purely philosophical to bricks and mortar. What is com-

Gus Jacccaci

mon is the interest in addressing community needs. As a futurist, Gus Jaccaci advises, "We need to get ahead of history and bring it to us. Social design and invention is one way to do this." The communiversities attending the meeting were dedicated to taking back their commu-

Joanne Jacccaci

nities, solving challenges such as energy independence, and sustainability in general including food supply and commerce. The Jaccacis are particularly concerned with species extinction, and with this poem penned by Gus Jaccaci, share their hope that cooperation within communities will help solve this problem:

CREATING COMMUNIVERSITIES
A Communiversity
Is a learning conversation
Within a whole family of life
In a place they hold in common
Dear to them all.

This conversation
Is a sharing of mutual needs
In a place of mutual dwelling
In a process of mutual learning
In a vessel of mutual hope.

This continuous conversation
Is the voice of the soul of life
Expressing the sanctity of all life
For the future of all life
In the home of all life.

Gus goes on to say:

Just when the governments of the world at all levels are torn in a struggle between greed and goodness, between social arrogance and sacred artistry, local communiversities and local neighborhoods are emerging as the new form of profitability, the new fulcrum of conscious evolution, and the new rejuvenated soul of society. Community, as in former times, is becoming the newborn working political economy most viable and powerful in the struggle for survival and salvation. Communiversity, where the whole community learns in partnership, is a critical component in an emerging global civilization.

Across the country, it's easy to see that we are experiencing a decay of local communities. The buildings remain but the glue that held them together has somehow vanished. Looking back, we can see how communities originally evolved around commercial cores such as manufacturing (the mill village), transportation hubs, retail/financial centers, and others. There's much discussion about the sustainability that includes our environment and the very existence of life. However that plays out, it seems to be clear that a new core will be required for the communities of the future. This time, however, that core is likely to be very different from those in the past. It has to be. The new core is likely to be composed of educational and creative resources that make up and grow out from the communiversity. In a way, communiversities are the starter dough for the "new loaf" of tomorrow's communities. Through education, innovation, and a renewed focus on "local," these communities will evolve, and in ways that are difficult to see today.

William H. Hale, Jr., of Athens, Georgia, is a master educator and one of the founding members of the University of Georgia Center for Continuing Education. Bill also is visionary and shares this insight on the ultimate manifestation of Featherbone Communiversity. In his view an entire city could consider itself a communiversity.

Bill Hale

Communiversity: Every Citizen a Student

Paraphrasing Thomas Jefferson, this nation is endowed by its creator with a spirit of learning. From the earliest times of the European settlement in the lands of the aboriginal Indians, a system of schools became the hallmark of American society. It took a while, but learning became a part of the nation's DNA. In this new thing called democracy, learning systems were devised as an essential component of society and it was not just for those who could afford it. Each hamlet, village or town first built roads, then a school, and this led to the spread of the amazing American public school.

It only takes a casual perusal of media today to see the obsession that people have with school and education. And with information, data and exciting news flowing all around us, it is impossible not to be a student if you live in this country. If someone famous did not say it, they should have: "One of the distinguishing characteristics of human beings is that they are learners."

If a community such as Gainesville/Hall County would declare itself, as a whole, the communiversity, that would be a bold and unique innovation—and an exciting step forward for learning and education. When we combine the two words, "community" and "university" into "communiversity," it becomes an idea larger than the two words could ever mean separately. Communiversity implies that every citizen is a student. Perhaps one of the first tasks of the communiversity is to reclaim the word "student" from its use by many as something in the past and make it an active word for life and learning in the future. Our "student" days are never over if we live in a city which is itself a communiversity. Learning in that sense becomes very much like a cloud that permeates the entire area.

For sure, communiversity is not a nebulous concept; it must have a locus, a place where curricula are engaged to meet the specific needs of the student. Featherbone Communiversity serves as an example. There are two brands of students in a communiversity, the "engaged" and the "to be engaged." One is overtly involved and the other is covertly involved. All the existing institutions which already promote learning as their primary activity will welcome the creation of an environment in which learning is an integral part of life and as pervasive as health or food.

Cities and towns across the nation strive to capture the essence of their given area by placing emphasis on the one thing that makes them distinctive. Dozens of examples come to mind. Some are known for their white sandy beaches, or their emphasis on the arts, or even the flower or food that proliferates there. So why cannot Gainesville/Hall County take on the patina of "learning"?

With that as a defining characteristic, what better place to live, grow and expand!

So, we're all endowed with a spirit of learning. It's in our DNA. Also in our DNA is the bias for local action; that's what has made America great from the beginning. In a way, communiversity brings us back to our roots and helps us reinvent our communities from the inside out. Featherbone Communiversity is an example of this phenomenon in action. There will be many others in the years ahead. I hope that you will remain open to the possibilities of communiversity in your life and your community.

Brenau Nursing students at Featherbone Communiversity

CHAPTER NINE

What's Next For You?

S o what's next for Warren Featherbone? Agriculture, banking, philanthropy, manufacturing, education (Featherbone Communiversity)...what's next? Of course I don't know for sure, but I believe the future will pull us to it if we stay open to who we are, not just what we've done. That's also where the opportunities are for you and me as individuals. I also believe hope is what's next, because hope is a choice, our choice.

Thank you for being a reader of this book and perhaps the entire Featherbone series, which began in 1996. Each of the three books was a remarkable journey of relationship building, discovery, and the sharing of knowledge and wisdom. What a great trip we've been on together. On this journey, what we've observed in the life of The Warren Featherbone Company is constant upheaval followed by new opportunities and change...since 1883. As a person whose career has been in the "business" for 40 years, I have been caught up in those changes, corporately and personally, just like you in your life and career. My privilege has been to narrate the journey and share with you lessons learned along the way.

What have we learned together on this trip? Well, many things of course. Transition has been discussed in each of the Featherbone books. As we close this book I'd like to focus on three attitudes that can help us through any transition: being grateful, being focused on serving, and being open to following our inherent gifts.

Gratitude

I've come to the conclusion that, though I appreciate my blessings, I haven't always been truly grateful. That kind of gratitude is deeper, more compelling, and focuses our conscious thought in a powerful way.

Over time, I have gone through periods of not sleeping well. Years in fact. Maybe you have too. We have lots of company. According to a 2008 Marketdata Enterprises, Inc. report, 58% of the U.S. population is estimated to experience insomnia symptoms or sleep disorders. The market for sleep aids of all types is $23.7 billion!

Not sleeping has almost become a badge of honor in our society. Not sleeping (not having time to sleep because we're so busy and important) means we're productive! Ego, with a sometimes distorted sense of self, often gets in the way of our being more productive, not to mention limiting relationships and sleep. Feeling the weight of the world on us is a big contributor too. Perhaps, we're worried about something. And, from time to time, that will be the case, but not every night. Recent health studies have shown that proper sleep is as important to our well-being as nutrition and exercise. We need to realistically see ourselves: assets and liabilities. We can develop the assets and work on the liabilities without obsessing on them. We have many gifts to share with others. Focus on the gifts.

I have found there really are no shortcuts to the restorative sleep we need. Over the years, I have tried every sleep aid known to medicine, and in certain situations they do help. But that's not the cure. One easy suggestion is to move your lighted alarm clock away from your bed. We don't need that reminder of time passing, or the light emitted. I have found something else to "chew on" at bedtime. I hope this mediation helps you too.

A Gratefulness Meditation

At the end of the day, sit in a place of quiet. Take a few minutes to review the day. Recall all the pleasant people and events, noting also those that were difficult or unpleasant.

Close your eyes and allow the significant people or events to arise one by one. Viewing the pleasant experiences, one at a time, let yourself give thanks for whichever gifts may have touched your life today. Silently name any gratefulness you may feel for each person or event, taking the time to let your heart open and receive the richness and nourishment of that experience. Let yourself appreciate and give thanks for each gift, allowing each image to arise and fade away until you feel complete.

Next, begin to recall any unpleasant experiences from the day. Focus your attention on one particularly painful encounter or event. Now, try to touch that memory with gratefulness. What do you notice as you practice giving thanks for something painful? What emotions arise? Does it make you peaceful or angry? Does it feel easy or hard? Stay with one image, repeatedly giving thanks for the fact that this person or event was part of your day. Be thankful for whatever teaching they brought, whatever they helped you notice about yourself. One by one, touch each memory with some gratefulness.

Finally, give thanks for your life. Take a moment to explicitly name all the qualities of your life for which you are grateful. Practice being thankful for your breath, your body, the people who care for you, your spouse, lover, children, friends, for the colors of the day, for your home, for your food. Reviewing as many gifts as come to mind, speak a word of silent thanksgiving for everything you have and for all that you have become.

—Author unknown

Service

Because of our unique gifts we will be called on to lead from time to time. You may not think of yourself as a leader because our culture has romanticized the term to imply that leadership is ego-centered. Actually the true nature of leadership in the highest sense is serving. And that's something we can intuitively embrace. When you find yourself in a position that can benefit from your leadership, find some way to serve ***those who will follow you.***

The Robert K. Greenleaf Center for Servant-Leadership was established in 1964 by Robert Greenleaf. Larry Spears served as President & CEO of The Greenleaf Center from 1990 to 2007. He is now President & CEO of The Spears Center for Servant-Leadership, established in 2008. In 1970, Robert K. Greenleaf published an essay, "The Servant as Leader." This ushered in the Servant-Leadership approach to leadership development that is used so often today. The concept of Servant-Leadership is thousands of years old and was articulated in the east by Lao Tzu (600 B.C.) and in the west by Jesus of Nazareth, and others. Mr. Spears highlights Greenleaf's definition of Servant-Leadership which says, "The best test (of servant-leadership), and difficult to administer, is: do those served grow as persons, do they grow while being served, become healthier, wiser, freer, more autonomous, more likely themselves to become servants?" Mr. Spears has further identified ten characteristics of the servant-leader: listening, empathy, healing, awareness, persuasion, conceptualization, foresight, stewardship, commitment to the growth of people, and building community.

10 Characteristics of a Servant-Leader

Reprinted courtesy of Larry C. Spears, The Spears Center for Servant-Leadership, Inc. (www.spearscenter.org).

Listening. Leaders have traditionally been valued for their communication and decision-making skills. While these are important skills for the servant-leader, they need to be reinforced by a deep commitment to listening intently to others. The servant-leader seeks to identify the will of the group and helps clarify that will. He or she seeks to listen receptively to what is being said. Listening, coupled with regular periods of reflection, is essential to the growth of the servant-leader.

Empathy. The servant-leader strives to understand and empathize with others. People need to be accepted and recognized for their special and unique spirits. One assumes the good intentions of co-workers and does not reject them as people, even if one finds it necessary to refuse to accept their behavior or performance.

Healing. One of the great strengths of servant-leadership is the potential for healing one's self and others. Many people have broken spirits and have suffered from a variety of emotional hurts. Although this is part of being human, servant-leaders recognize they also have the opportunity to "help make whole" those with whom they come in contact. In the "Servant as Leader" Greenleaf writes: "There is something subtle communicated to one who is being served and led if implicit in the compact between the servant-leader and led is the understanding that the search for wholeness is something they share."

AWARENESS. General awareness, and especially self-awareness, strengthens the servant-leader. Awareness also aids one in understanding issues involving ethics and values. It lends itself to being able to view most situations from a more integrated, holistic position. As Greenleaf observed: "Awareness is not a giver of solace—it is just the opposite. It is a disturber and an awakener. Able leaders are usually sharply awake and reasonably disturbed. They are not seekers after solace. They have their own serenity."

PERSUASION. Another characteristic of servant-leaders is a primary reliance on persuasion rather than positional authority in making decisions within an organization. The servant-leader seeks to convince others rather than coerce compliance. This particular element offers one of the clearest distinctions between the traditional authoritarian model and that of servant-leadership. The servant-leader is effective at building consensus within groups.

CONCEPTUALIZATION. Servant-leaders seek to nurture their abilities to "dream great dreams." The ability to look at a problem (or an organization) from a conceptualizing perspective means that one must think beyond day-to-day realities. For many managers this is a characteristic that requires discipline and practice. Servant-leaders are called to serve a delicate balance between conceptual thinking and a day-to-day focused approach.

FORESIGHT. Foresight is a characteristic that enables the servant-leader to understand the lessons from the past, the realities of the present, and the likely consequence of a decision for the future. It is also deeply rooted within the intuitive mind. Foresight remains a largely unexplored area in leadership studies, but one most deserving of careful attention.

STEWARDSHIP. Peter Block has defined stewardship as "holding something in trust for another." Robert Greenleaf's view of all institutions is one in which CEO's, staffs, and trustees all played significant roles in holding their institutions in trust for the greater good of society. Servant-leadership, like stewardship, assumes first and foremost a commitment to serving the needs of others. It also emphasizes the use of openness and persuasion rather than control.

COMMITMENT TO THE GROWTH OF PEOPLE. Servant-leaders believe that people have an intrinsic value beyond their tangible contributions as workers. As a result, the servant-leader is deeply committed to the growth of each and every individual within the institution. The servant-leader recognizes the tremendous responsibility to do everything possible to nurture the growth of employees.

BUILDING COMMUNITY. The servant-leader senses that much has been lost in recent human history as a result of the shift from local communities to large institutions as the primary shaper of human lives. This awareness causes the servant-leader to seek to identify some means of building community among those who work within a given institution. Servant-leadership suggests that this community can be created among those who work in businesses and other institutions. Greenleaf said: "All that is needed to rebuild community as a viable life form for large numbers of people is for enough servant-leaders to show the way, not by mass movements, but by each servant-leader demonstrating his own unlimited liability for a quite specific community-related group."

Being open to our gifts

"Leap and the net will appear." Or, as my friend Walt Boomershine says, "S-T-A-R-T!" We have to move! Even if we fall, let's fall forward. We must trust ourselves and be open to what's in our DNA.

In my last book, *The Gift of Renewal*, I related a very powerful quote: "Children are living messages we send to a time we will not see." That helps us more deeply appreciate the responsibility we have to our children today as they are "our messages" to the future. But let's take this thought even further. WE are the messages sent to this time by all those who have gone before us. They have given us unique talents and gifts. Are WE stepping up? What do we fear?

Author Marianne Williamson writes: *Our deepest fear is not that we are inadequate. Our deepest fear is that we are powerful beyond measure. It is our light, not our darkness, that most frightens us. We ask ourselves, who am I to be brilliant, gorgeous, talented, fabulous? Actually, who are you not to be? You are a child of God. Your playing small doesn't serve the world.*

There's nothing enlightened about shrinking so that other people won't feel insecure around you. We are meant to shine as children do. We are born to make manifest the glory of God that is within us. It's not just in some of us; it's in everyone. And as we let our own light shine, we unconsciously give other people permission to do the same. As we are liberated from our own fear, our presence automatically liberates others.

When we use those talents we are operating in an environment where we do not need to fear competition. Since we are using our unique gifts, the competition isn't there. If we aren't using our unique gifts, the competition is everywhere! Also, I have found that when odds are the smallest they often are best. Why? Because in those situations the "competition" stays home!

Give what you love to do! That's your unique gift. Ask yourself this question: "If my career vanished today and I had to select another (for which I probably would not be paid), what would it be?" Do that for a living! Remembering that if you are "hooked at the roots" with your family, friends, and community, you will be ready to take that leap of faith. And the net will appear.

Before we go...
Live in the moment!
Yesterday is a cancelled check.
Tomorrow is a promissory note.
Today is cold cash.

It is amazing to me that so many of our days are spent thinking about the past or future. We worry about both and can do absolutely nothing about either. We have only the present moment. And in that present moment, we have everything we need to deal with it. There is no worry in now.

Let's stay in touch. Over the years I have met truly remarkable people through these books and presentations I have made around the country. Many of those people have shared their stories, their leaps of faith, and their discoveries. Let's continue the conversation. I'd love to hear your story. Please email gwhalen@ngcf.org.

What's next for you?
Hope. It's our choice...always.

Oseola McCarty

CHAPTER TEN

Final Thoughts

*F*eatherbone Communiversity has been made possible through the financial support of many wonderful people. Gifts have been large and small, thousands of them, all contributing to the service provided by the organizations you have met in this book. These final thoughts are dedicated to giving and the potential that we all have to give and change America in the process.

The Power to Give

"Community" starts with one, and one woman who personified being a blessing to others in a big way was Oseola McCarty. She worked all her life washing and ironing other people's clothes. She didn't earn much, but she always saved her money. Her one regret was that she had little education, for she had quit school to help her family. In 1995 at age 87 she did an amazing thing: she gave $150,000 to the University of Southern Mississippi, located in her home town, so other young people could afford to stay in school. Oseola McCarty was a woman who loved the Lord and loved to give.

Don't you find the most generous people often come from modest backgrounds? They give because it's the right thing to do. Sharing is a way to express themselves. Famous psychologist and philosopher, Erich Fromm, has written, "Giving is the highest expression of potency. In the very act of giving I experience my strength, my wealth, my power." And so it is with all of us—we give because our giving does good and is good for us.

Philanthropy is often misunderstood. The word itself can be confusing...too close to the word philanderer! Philanthropy refers to investments we make in society. I like the way Claire Gaudiani, author of The Greater Good says it. "Some think America is generous because it is rich. The truth is that America is rich because it is generous." And America has been generous for a very long time.

My great-grandfather, E.K. Warren, was a philanthropist even when he had little money. Five years before he founded The Warren Featherbone Company he had already purchased Warren Woods, the pristine forest that became a state park. So it appears he had the heart before he had the resources. Years later, in 1917, he organized the first foundation in Michigan before there was a Kellogg Foundation, a Ford Foundation, or any others. His concept ushered in an era of corporate giving that has been largely responsible for building the America we know today. The Warren Featherbone Foundation, successor to the E.K. Warren Foundation, seeks to now democratize philanthropy through an initiative known as "401P" and the creation of Personal Philanthropy Accounts.

This idea came to us in 2005 and is based on significant shortcomings in the present tax code. We have even filed a patent for this "business process", but have done so principally to promote the idea.

My friends, Andrew and Emily Dorisio, are husband and wife and Patent and Tax attorneys respectively. They have clearly articulated shortcomings in our current tax system.

The current tax system provides no real incentive for early and generous charitable deductions. Rather, it simply allows taxpayers to re-collect the contributions made during the past year at tax time (which typically involves poring over checkbook stubs, credit card records and cash receipts) and then apply complicated, sometimes unworkable, rules to determine the appropriate deduction available. This is deleterious for the taxpayer.

The disincentive created by the required record-keeping and complicated rules breeds a second problem: widespread abuse of the deduction under the current system. Unless uncovered during infrequently conducted and costly audits (which usually are not cost-justified in view of the amount of under-reporting typically involved), the IRS simply cannot determine the veracity of the taxpayer as to any deductions for claimed charitable contributions. This is deleterious for the government.

A third problem created by current law is the availability of the deduction only to taxpayers who itemize deductions (which estimates place at only one-fourth of all taxpayers). Accordingly, millions of American taxpayers cannot deduct charitable contributions, and thus have no incentive to make same. This is deleterious for the charitable organizations.

So, the U.S. has a tax system that discourages charitable donations for the majority of taxpayers and has an adverse effect on both government and charitable organizations. To address this, Congressman Nathan Deal (R-GA) introduced legislation in 2005 in the U.S. House of Representatives, which would create personal philanthropy accounts. In 2006, Senators Johnny Isakson and Saxby Chambliss (R-GA) joined him in the U.S. Senate. In 2009, support continues to build for passage of this important legislation. In their own words Senator Isakson and Congressman Deal tell us why they have introduced Personal Philanthropy Account legislation into both houses of Congress.

SENATOR JOHNNY ISAKSON

In June 2007, Senator Chambliss and I introduced S. 1568, the Personal Philanthropy Account Act. I believe that personal philanthropy accounts will offer all Americans the opportunity to make a real impact on the charity of their choice, to leave a lasting legacy to their community, and to benefit our nation as a whole.

I believe this legislation will encourage more Americans to donate to charitable organizations by allowing donors to receive immediate tax benefits for their contributions. The personal philanthropy accounts created by this legislation will allow all contributions to grow tax-free and then be distributed to charities without ever being taxed.

Also, I designed the legislation to be beneficial to employers by allowing them to have the option of matching their employees' contributions to their personal philanthropy accounts. This matching would be a tax-deductible business expense in the same way that employers can match employees' contributions to their 401(K) retirement account. This enables the account to grow faster and gives employers a tax incentive to become involved in the charities their employees care about.

Congressman Nathan Deal

H.R. 2000 provides an effective tool to stimulate all Americans regardless of wealth to become active in philanthropies, which benefit their individual communities as well as our nation. No longer would an individual be prohibited from giving on the basis of income, and combined with employer matching contributions, larger donations could be made over time.

By allowing these accounts to grow tax-free and be distributed without ever being taxed, much needed funding will reach those organizations to which it is intended, not siphoned into Washington for the benefit of the federal government.

Here specifically is what Congress is considering in the Personal Philanthropy Account legislation and, with your help, this can become law.

What is a Personal Philanthropy Account?

A Personal Philanthropy Account (PPA) is a financial planning tool which allows individuals to receive an "above the line" tax deduction for future charitable contributions and allows these funds to grow in a tax-free account, so individuals can make larger, more meaningful donations over time.

How does it work?

Through a PPA, individuals can utilize an automatic deduction from their paycheck before their income tax is calculated and withheld. These deducted amounts would accumulate and earn interest over time.

The amount of the tax deduction would be equal to the amount of cash contributions made to the account by the individual or on the individual's behalf during the year.

Employers have the option of matching their employee's contributions to their PPA. This matching would be a tax-deductible business expense in the same way that employers can match an employee's contributions to their 401k retirement account. This enables the account to grow twice as fast and gives employers a tax incentive to become involved in the charities their employees care about.

Why are they needed?
Currently, only people who itemize their deductions have a tax incentive to make charitable contributions. Unfortunately, these individuals only make up around 26% of the population. PPA's provide the other 74% of the population, who take the standard deduction, with a tax incentive to give to charity through this tax free account.

Empowering this large segment of the population would result in an enormous increase in the amount of money given to charitable organizations, which are far more efficient than the government at serving many of the needs of society.

Conditions

No minimum annual donation from the account would be required for accounts with a balance under $10,000. For accounts with a balance of $10,000 or more, a minimum donation amount of 5% of the account balance must be made to qualified charitable organizations each fiscal year.

Charitable organizations eligible to receive donations are all non-profit groups that qualify under section 501(c)(3) of the U.S. Tax code. As stated in section 501(c)(3), such an organization's function must be for either charitable, religious, educational, scientific, or literary purposes, or have the central goal of testing for public safety, fostering national or international amateur sports competition, or the prevention of cruelty to children or animals.

Conclusion

U.S. House and Senate legislation amends the IRS tax code to allow for the creation of Personal Philanthropy Accounts.

PPA's empower all citizens, regardless of income, to make a real impact on the charity of their choice, to leave a lasting legacy to their community, and to benefit our nation as a whole, all without adding to the size of the federal government.

As noted earlier, E.K. Warren ushered in the era of corporate giving through foundations, and today there are approximately 70,000 foundations in America. Democratizing philanthropy through "401P" Personal Philanthropy Accounts will in effect create a new world of millions of "one-person foundations". In the tradition of Oseola McCarty, these individuals will be better able to tell their stories through giving.

"I am only one, but I am one..." That is the spirit that brings about changes for the greater good.

About the Author

Charles E. "Gus" Whalen, Jr., is Chairman of The Warren Featherbone Company established in 1883. Through the years Warren Companies have been engaged in manufacturing, banking, agriculture, philanthropy and education. In 1993, Gus Whalen re-established the Warren Featherbone Foundation, originally founded in 1917, to increase public awareness of the importance of interdependent connections in business and society. His first three books, *The Featherbone Principle: A Declaration of Interdependence*, *The Featherbone Spirit: Celebrating Life's Connections*, and *The Gift of Renewal* have reached a wide audience. Gus is frequently invited to speak to diverse audiences including corporations, associations, educators and government groups.

Acknowledgements

This book has been made possible through the collective efforts, talents and inspiration of some truly gifted individuals. I want you to meet them and know how much I appreciate the investment they have made in this work.

Phil Bellury—gifted writer, researcher and collaborator of this our fourth book

Nell Whalen—my wife and life partner of nearly 42 years, master editor and compiler of the introduction of EK Warren's life.

The creative team:

        Laurie Shock—Book designer
        Larry Griffeth—Photographer
        Billy Howard—Photographer
        Rudi Kiefer—Photographer
        Robb Maag—Photographer
        Dave Simpson—Photographer

My co-editors and contributors:

David L. Bond—National Career Pathways Network—Waco, Texas

Harris Blackwood—*The Times*—Gainesville, GA

Chris Cosper—Gainesville, GA

Congressman Nathan Deal—Ninth District of Georgia

Lloyd E. (Pete) Fleming—United States Department of Labor—Atlanta, GA

William H. Hale, Jr.—Retired administrator, University of Georgia—Athens, GA

Sheri Hooper—Interactive Neighborhood for Kids (INK)—Gainesville, GA

Marsha Hopkins—Gainesville, GA

Gus and Joanne Jaccaci—Unity Scholars—New Gloucester, ME

Lee Lathrop—Vancouver, WA

Jim Mathis—North GA Community Foundation—Gainesville, GA

James E. Mathis, Sr.—Gainesville, GA

Dr. Mike Moye—Lanier Technical College—Oakwood, GA

Dr. Martha Nesbitt—Gainesville State College—Oakwood, GA

Mary Ann Rojas—Workforce Solutions of the Coastal Bend—Corpus Christi, Texas

B. David Rowe—LaGrange College—LaGrange, GA

Will Schofield—Hall County Schools—Gainesville, GA

Dr. Ed Schrader—Brenau University—Gainesville, GA

Dr. Carroll Turner—Lanier Technical College Manufacturing Development Center—Gainesville, GA